THEMATIC UNIT
FLIGHT

Written by Judy Vaden

Illustrated by Sue Fullam and Keith Vasconcelles

Teacher Created Materials, Inc.
6421 Industry Way
Westminster, CA 92683
www.teachercreated.com
©1991 Teacher Created Materials, Inc
Reprinted, 2002
Made in U.S.A.
ISBN-1-55734-281-4

Table of Contents

Introduction

Flight contains a captivating, whole language, thematic unit about the development of flight. Its 80 exciting, reproducible pages are filled with a wide variety of lesson ideas designed for use with intermediate children. At its core are four high quality literature selections. Each piece includes activities which set the stage for reading, encourage reading enjoyment, and help students apply the concepts they learn through reading to daily life. In addition, the theme is interwoven with activities across the curriculum in language arts, writing, math, social studies, science, and art. Many of these activities encourage cooperative learning. Suggestions and patterns for bulletin boards and unit management tools are additional time savers for the busy teacher. Highlighting this complete teacher resource are two culminating activities: "A Day at the Airplane Races" and *Challenges*, a student play. These activities allow students to synthesize and apply their knowledge beyond the classroom.

This thematic unit includes:

❑ **literature selections**—summaries of three books and a poem with related activities

❑ **writing ideas**—daily suggestions, including Big Books, for writing across the curriculum

❑ **social studies activities**—a historical journey from Leonardo da Vinci to the *Voyager*

❑ **science experiments**—hands-on discoveries about why airplanes fly

❑ **curriculum connections**—language arts, math, science, social studies, art, and life skills like career awareness

❑ **group projects**—to foster cooperative learning

❑ **bulletin board ideas**—suggestions and plans for student-created and/or interactive bulletin boards

❑ **planning guides**—suggestions for sequencing lessons each day of the unit

❑ **culminating activities**—to help students synthesize their learning

❑ **bibliography**—suggestions for additional books on the theme

---

To keep this valuable resource intact so that it can be used year after year, you may wish to punch holes in the pages and store them in a three–ring binder.

Introduction *(cont.)*

Why Whole Language?

A whole language approach involves children in using all modes of communication: reading, writing, listening, observing, illustrating, experiencing, and doing. Communication skills are interconnected and integrated into lessons that emphasize the whole of language rather than isolating its parts. The lessons revolve around selected literature. Reading is not taught as a separate subject from writing and spelling, for example. A child reads, writes, speaks, listens, and thinks in response to a literature experience introduced by the teacher. In this way, language skills grow naturally, stimulated by involvement and interest in the topic at hand.

Why Thematic Planning?

One very useful tool for implementing an integrated whole language program is thematic planning. By choosing a theme with correlating literature selections for a unit of study, a teacher can plan activities throughout the day that lead to a cohesive, in-depth study of the topic. Students will be practicing and applying their skills in meaningful contexts. Consequently, they will tend to learn and retain more. Both teachers and students will be freed from a day that is broken into unrelated segments of isolated drill and practice.

Why Cooperative Learning?

Besides academic skills and content, students need to learn social skills. No longer can this area of development be taken for granted. Students must learn to work cooperatively in groups in order to function well in modern society. Group activities should be a regular part of school life and teachers should consciously include social objectives as well as academic objectives in their planning. The teacher should clarify and monitor the qualities of good group interaction just as he/she would clarify and monitor the academic goals of the project.

Why Big Books?

An excellent cooperative, whole language activity is the production of Big Books. Groups of students, or the whole class, can apply their language skills, content knowledge, and creativity to produce a Big Book that can become a part of the classroom library to be read and reread. These books make excellent culminating projects for sharing beyond the classroom with parents, librarians, other classes, etc. Big Books can be produced in many ways and this thematic unit book includes directions for at least one method you may choose.

"Wilbur Wright and Orville Wright"

by Rosemary and Stephen Vincent Benét

Said Orville Wright to Wilbur Wright,
"These birds are very trying.
I'm sick of hearing them cheep-cheep
About the fun of flying.
A bird has feathers, it is true.
That much I freely grant.
But must that stop us, W?"
Said Wilbur Wright, "It shan't."

And so they built a glider, first,
And then they built another.
—There never were two brothers more
Devoted to each other.
They ran a dusty little shop
For bicycle-repairing,
And bought each other soda-pop
And praised each other's daring.

They glided here, they glided there,
They sometimes skinned their noses,
—For learning how to rule the air
Was not a bed of roses—
But each would murmur, afterward,
While patching up his bro,
"Are we discouraged, W?"
"Of course we are not, O!"

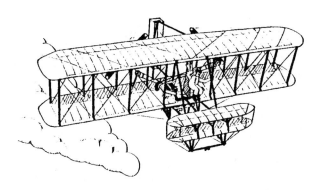

And finally, at Kitty Hawk
In Nineteen-Three (let's cheer it!),
The first real airplane really flew
With Orville there to steer it!
—And kingdoms may forget their kings
And dogs forget their bites,
But, not till Man forgets his wings,
Will men forget the Wrights.

From *A Book of Americans* by Rosemary and Stephen Vincent Benét (Holt, Rinehart and Winston, Inc., 1933 by Stephen Vincent Benét. Copyright renewed).

©1961 by Rosemary Carr Benét. Reprinted by permission of Brandt & Brandt Literary Agents, Inc.)

"Wilbur Wright and Orville Wright" *(cont.)*

The outline below is a suggested plan for using the various activities that are presented in this unit. You should adapt these ideas to fit your own classroom situation.

Sample Plan

Day 1

- Cluster information known about the Wright brothers
- Read the poem (page 5)
- Vocabulary activities (page 41)
- Introduce Scientific Method (page 52)
- Students choose books to read about the Wright brothers (page 80)
- 15 minutes of Super Quiet Reading Time: SQRT (page 7)
- Math activity—Flying High (page 49)

Day 2

- Introduce Taking Notes (page 8)
- Read information from the encyclopedia; have class practice taking notes
- SQRT
- Science experiment—Lift (page 54)
- Daily Writing Topics (page 28)

Day 3

- Reread the poem
- SQRT
- Have students read together as partners

- Continue Daily Writing Topics
- Continue Vocabulary Activities
- Art Activity (page 64)
- Introduce Wright Brothers' Biography (page 9)

Day 4

- Continue Daily Writing Topics
- SQRT
- Leonardo da Vinci biography (page 10)
- Partner reading
- Write letters for information (page 28)

Day 5

- Reread the poem
- Continue Daily Writing Topics
- SQRT
- Math activity—Altitude Graph (page 50)
- Summary discussion about the Wright brothers

Overview of Activities

Setting the Stage

1. Prepare your classroom for a unit on flight. Collect books and magazines about planes, flying, inventors, and aviators. See page 80 for suggestions. Put up an appropriate bulletin board like Up, Up and Away, page 71. Use clip art on pages 75-78.

2. Record on chart paper what the class knows about the topic of flight. Later write down more information in other colors. This helps students see how much they have learned during the unit.

Overview of Activities *(cont.)*

3. Introduce note-taking techniques (page 8). Emphasize "clue words" which trigger a string of ideas. Discuss the importance of taking just enough notes to understand the information a week later. Read information from an encyclopedia to the class and have them practice taking notes. Have students write only one word or phrase on each line of their papers or on 3" x 5" cards. Have students sort facts into topics.

4. Super Quiet Reading Time (SQRT). Plan a 15-20 minute period each day for SQRT. Have each student read a book about the Wright brothers. See page 80 for examples. Have students take notes on the books they are reading. Give 15 minutes of reading homework, and set a date for books to be finished.

5. Discuss the questions at the bottom of page 10, and have students read the Leonardo da Vinci biography.

6. Discuss what makes a good scientist. Introduce the scientific method and experiment form, pages 52 and 53.

7. Begin science experiments, pages 54-57. Use the experiment cards to make a science center in your classroom.

8. Begin vocabulary activities (page 41).

Enjoying the Poem

1. Have students read the poem several times. Have them read orally, silently, with a partner or in chorus. Discuss the importance of looking for new insights with each reading.

2. Begin Daily Writing Topics (page 28).

3. Describe to the class how the Wright brothers loved to read. (They often read aloud to each other and argued about topics they read. They particularly liked reading science books and the encyclopedia.) Assign reading partners and give each pair an encyclopedia to read together. Have students continue this activity throughout the unit.

4. Discuss how the Wright brothers found information by writing letters to informed sources like the Smithsonian Institution and the National Oceanic and Atmospheric Administration (U.S. Weather Bureau), and by talking personally with experts in a field. Have students write to several different sources for information about something which interests them. (See page 28 for addresses.)

5. Display student work on We Meet the Challenge! bulletin board. (See page 72 for ideas.)

Extending the Poem

1. After students have finished reading their books on the Wright Brothers, divide the class into groups for oral discussion of questions on page 9. Students may use their notes. To help students contribute to the discussion, give each one a sheet of colored paper. When a student contributes, have him/her place the paper in the center of the group. When all papers are in the center, begin the next round by giving the sheets back to the students when they give their answers. This method assures that each student will participate in the discussion.

2. Have students organize their notes from their books into different topics: education, family background, disappointments, hobbies. The next day have students write a paragraph about each topic.

Taking Notes

Organize the information into the two categories provided. First, write "clue words" for each sentence in the space provided. "Clue words" are important words that remind you of a whole idea or sentence. Then write your "clue words" in the correct categories. The first two are done for you.

1. The *Kitty Hawk Flyer* weighed 605 pounds without the pilot. _____ *airplane weight* _____

2. On the third flight Orville flew 200 feet and stayed aloft for 15 seconds. ____ *15-second flight* ____

3. On Friday, December 17, 1903 at Kitty Hawk, North Carolina, the Wright Brothers were successful in their goal. _____

4. There were two counter-rotating propellers made of laminated spruce wood._____

5. The fourth and final flight was the longest and farthest._____

6. The wood was covered with canvas and painted with aluminum paint. _____

7. Wilbur flew 175 feet for 12 seconds. _____

8. The propellers turned 330 revolutions per minute and produced 90 pounds of thrust. _____

9. There were four flights that day. _____

10. The engine was made of four iron cylinders which produced 12 horsepower._____

11. Wilbur provided the flight control by lying prone on the lower wing._____

12. It was 21 feet long and the wingspan was 40 feet, 4 inches. _____

13. The horizontal elevators were moved up and down by his left hand._____

14. Orville flew 120 feet and the flight lasted 12 seconds._____

About the Flight	About the *Kitty Hawk Flyer*

Biography

A biography is a book which describes the life of a person. Read a biography of the Wright brothers. There are several from which to choose on page 80. Answer as many questions below as possible:

1. Describe Wilbur and Orville's family.

2. Describe a typical day from Wilbur and Orville's childhood.

3. Reading was very important to the Wright brothers. Describe some events from the book which prove this. Tell how reading affected their lives.

4. Name 3 sources the Wright brothers used to find out more about a topic they wanted to understand.

5. Describe the airplane models the Wright brothers tried and changed before their successful flight.

6. At first, Wilbur and Orville based their experiments on facts discovered by another person. Who was this person? What valuable lesson did the brothers learn from this person?

Orville Wright

7. What was the main problem the brothers had to overcome in order to fly?

8. How did the brothers decide who would be the first to fly?

9. Describe the events of the first flight.

10. How did the newspapers react to this event?

11. How did the Wright brothers' invention affect the world?

12. Did other students get the same answers you did to these questions? Why or why not?

Wilbur Wright

Leonardo da Vinci

Leonardo da Vinci was born April 15, 1452, in Vinci, Italy. Attaining knowledge was his life goal. He studied and read books constantly. Leonardo did many experiments and took many notes and sketches. Accuracy in observation and measurement were of utmost importance to him. All his notes were in code so no one could steal his ideas. They were written in mirror writing which means everything was written backwards. Leonardo could write simultaneously with both hands, one writing forward and one writing backward. He was also an outstanding painter. Some of Leonardo's most famous paintings include *The Mona Lisa, The Last Supper,* and *The Virgin and Child with Saint Anne.* He also was a sculptor, architect, poet, musician, and engineer. He designed bridges, weapons, costumes, machines, and scientific instruments.

He also designed a parachute, helicopter, and ornithopter, a machine designed to fly by flapping its wings. His flying machines were actually built later when materials and equipment to build them became available. While knowledge was Leonardo's life goal, flying like a bird was his dream. He was never able to fly, but his dream became a reality 455 years later.

Underline key words from above. Answer the following questions in your own words after discussing the answers with your teacher.

1. Did Leonardo accomplish his goal?

2. Name two of Leonardo's works of art.

3. Leonardo da Vinci is often described as a universal man. Define the word "universal." Do you agree with this description of Leonardo?

4. How did Leonardo da Vinci influence the development of flight? Should he be given any credit along with the Wright brothers?

5. What indications were there that Leonardo knew how extraordinary his ideas were?

The Glorious Flight

by Alice and Martin Provensen

Summary

Louis Blériot was a pioneering force in the development of aviation. His flight across the English Channel showed the world that the airplane could go anywhere.

The outline below is a suggested plan for using the various activities that are presented in this unit. You should adapt these ideas to fit your own classroom situation.

Sample Plan

Day 1

- Discuss "Failure "
- Partner reading (page 7)
- Super Quiet Reading Time (SQRT) (page 7)
- Science experiments—Gravity (page 55)
- Read *The Glorious Flight*
- Make a class book about planes (pages 30-36)

Day 2

- Have students read for information (See Extending the Book, page 12)
- SQRT
- Daily Writing Topics (page 28)
- Vocabulary Activity (page 41)
- Louis Blériot biography (page 13)
- Math Activity—Airplane Measurement (page 45)

Day 3

- Reread the story
- Milestones in Flight History (page 58)
- SQRT

- Continue Daily Writing Topics
- Charles Lindbergh Biography (page 15)
- Math activity—Find Your Weight! (page 51)
- Make a book about Flight Careers (page 65)

Day 4

- SQRT
- News Story (page 14)
- Continue Daily Writing Topics
- Science experiment—Thrust (page 56)
- Illustrating reports (page 62)
- Flight Time Line (page 59)

Day 5

- Reread the story
- SQRT
- Continue Flight Time Line (page 59)
- Continue Daily Writing Topics
- Vocabulary Activity
- Art Activity (page 64)
- Venn Diagram (page 16)

Overview of Activities

Setting the Stage

1. Write the word "FAILURE" on the blackboard. Cluster and discuss students' ideas. Focus on students' feelings. Is failure ever beneficial? Why? When?

2. Have students write a paragraph about a time when they failed.

Enjoying the Book

1. Tell the class that *The Glorious Flight* is a true story about a person who failed.

2. Read the book. Discuss the question: "Was Louis Blériot a failure?"

3. Read the biography of Louis Blériot (page 13). Have students highlight or underline important facts. Have students take notes and write a news article about his flight. (See page 14.)

4. Charles Lindbergh was a great influence in the development of flight. Have students read the Lindbergh Biography, page 15. Have students look for pictures of his airplane and its specifications: length, wingspan, type of engine, maximum air speed, etc. They may wish to write a letter to the Smithsonian Institution for this information. (See page 28 for the address.)

Extending the Book

1. Teach students how to read an encyclopedia for important information. Pass out encyclopedias and have them read all bold, dark print first. Second, have them examine pictures and their captions. Third, have students study any charts or graphs. Fourth, have them read text and look for key words. Give students 10-15 minutes to find 5 facts about a topic and prepare a one-minute report for the class.

2. Do the Milestones and Time Line activity on pages 58 and 59.

3. Have students do book reports with illustrations. See page 62 for illustration techniques.

4. Make a class book about kinds of planes (see pages 30–36).

5. Have students write a book about Flight Careers, page 65.

Louis Blériot

Louis Blériot (bla ryo) was born in Cambrai, France on July 1, 1872. He invented and manufactured automobile lights as well as other automobile accessories. His success as an inventor enabled him to pursue his interest in aviation.

The first airplane Louis Blériot built was so small no one could sit in it. Over the next few years, Blériot designed, built and tested many planes. Each time the plane failed, he redesigned it, rebuilt it, and flew it again and again. Despite more than fifty failures, he continued to improve and try his designs.

Finally, when Louis had finished the Blériot XI, he felt he had designed the perfect airplane. This model had a long, enclosed body, a tail for rear control, and wheels for landing gear. The wing span was 25 feet 7 inches, and the plane weighed 484 pounds. The plane could fly 40 miles per hour. The London Daily Mail was offering 1000 pounds to the first person to fly across the English Channel. Louis Blériot thought this plane could make the flight.

On July 25, 1909 Louis Blériot took off from Les Baraques, France at 4:35 a.m. He headed in the direction of England. During his flight he became lost for ten minutes. He had no idea where he was because he had no compass. Louis' airplane engine also overheated, and if it had not been cooled by a rainstorm, Blériot would have crashed, failing once again.

Twenty-three miles and thirty-seven minutes later at 5:12 a.m. on July 25, 1909, he landed near Dover Castle, England. He had become the first international flyer! Louis' planes were soon in great demand, and he became a leading airplane manufacturer. Louis Blériot died in Paris, France on May 25, 1927.

News Story

News reporters use five W's to relate information clearly and quickly. In a newspaper, space is limited, so important facts are told first and details are added later. Using the five W's below, write a news story about Blériot (page 13) or Lindbergh (page 15). Create an exciting headline that will capture your readers' interest.

Who: _____

Where: _____ When: _____

What happened: _____

_____

_____

Why: _____

_____

Extra Details: _____

_____

Write your news story here.

_____
Headline

_____

_____

_____

_____

_____

_____

_____

_____

Charles Lindbergh

Charles Lindbergh was born on February 4, 1902, in Detroit, Michigan. As a child Lindbergh had exceptional mechanical ability. He had an early fascination with flying. After two years of college he left to become a barnstormer, a pilot who performed daredevil stunts at fairs. As an adult he pursued his dream by becoming a Reserve pilot in the U.S. Army where he developed a reputation for being a cautious yet capable flyer.

In 1927 Charles accepted the challenge to be the first aviator to fly across the Atlantic Ocean by himself. Many pilots had been killed or injured trying to cross the Atlantic, and none had ever succeeded. Charles planned extensively for his flight across the Atlantic. A special plane was built that had many fuel tanks. In fact, there was barely enough room for Lindbergh in the plane! He even had to use a periscope to see where he was going. Besides lots of fuel, the only things Charles took with him were two canteens of water, five ham sandwiches, and a compass. Before his historic flight, Charles practiced staying awake for many hours in order to simulate the real flying conditions he would experience.

On May 20, 1927, Lindbergh took off in his *Spirit of St. Louis* from Roosevelt Field, near New York City. Thirty-three and a half hours later, averaging a speed of 107 miles per hour, he landed at Le Bourget Field, near Paris, France. Thousands of people cheered as he arrived from his 3,600-mile journey. Charles had gained international fame for his feat, and the press nicknamed him "Lucky Lindy." More importantly, he had achieved his dream to be the first to fly solo across the Atlantic Ocean.

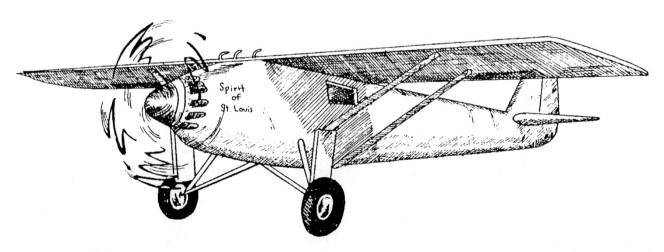

Venn Diagram

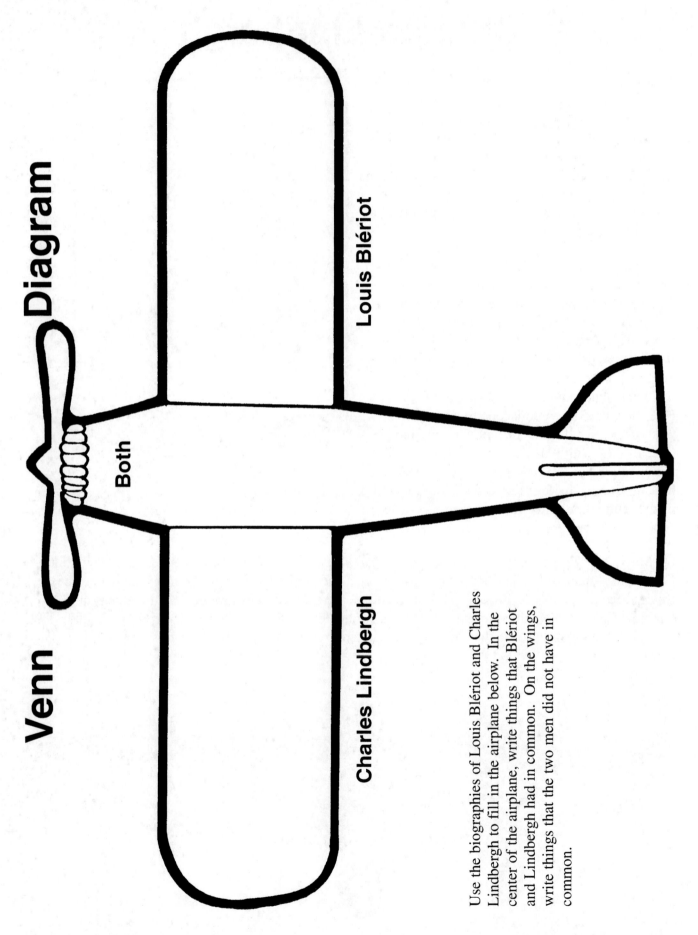

Louis Blériot

Both

Charles Lindbergh

Use the biographies of Louis Blériot and Charles Lindbergh to fill in the airplane below. In the center of the airplane, write things that Blériot and Lindbergh had in common. On the wings, write things that the two men did not have in common.

Lost Star

by Patricia Lauber

Summary

Amelia Earhart was not only influential in the development of flight, but also in encouraging women to do their best in whatever interested them. Amelia lived in a time when girls were limited by society in what they could do. Girls didn't wear pants, climb trees, or aspire to do anything more than get married and raise a family. Amelia's mother, however, believed that her daughters could and should do whatever they found interesting and challenging. Amelia's childhood adventures helped her to pursue her dream to fly.

The outline below is a suggested plan for using the various activities that are presented in this unit. You should adapt these ideas to fit your own classroom situation.

Sample Plan

Day 1

- Read pages 1-24
- 15 minutes of Super Quiet Reading Time: SQRT (page 7)
- Airplane Parts (page 44)
- Vocabulary Activity (page 41)
- Fact Pyramid (page 39)
- Memory Photo Album (page 22)

Day 2

- Read pages 25-44
- Amelia's Childhood (page 20)
- SQRT
- Daily Writing Topics
- Science experiment—Drag (page 57)
- Code Messages (page 43)
- Coast to Coast (page 48)

Day 3

- Read pages 45-65
- SQRT
- Continue Daily Writing Topics
- Art activity (page 64)

Day 4

- Read pages 66-80
- SQRT
- Continue Daily Writing Topics
- Continue Vocabulary Activities
- Voyager (page 38)

Day 5

- Finish the book
- SQRT
- Continue Daily Writing Topics
- Around the World (page 60)
- Begin Extending the Book activities (page 19)
- Last Flight (page 21)

Overview of Activities

Setting the Stage

1. Read pages 1–4 in Lost Star. Have a discussion with the class about the limitations put on women. Make up some limitations for the girls in the class. Ask them how they would feel if they could not play any active games like soccer, tag, or climbing the jungle gym. Ask the opinions of the boys in the class, discussing also the limitations sometimes placed on men.

2. Ask the girls what they want to do when they are adults. Discuss the kinds of jobs they can do and list them on the board. Ask students how would they feel if someone told them they couldn't do these jobs.

3. Discuss the restrictions Amelia Earhart faced when growing up. Explain that Amelia had to fight to do what she wanted all her life, and because of her efforts, girls and boys today have more freedom to do the things they want.

Enjoying the Book

1. Read and discuss pages 5–24 in *Lost Star*. Have students describe Amelia's childhood and do page 20. Explain how and why it was different from other children. How did Amelia's mother influence her? How did her father and his drinking problem influence her? Discuss problems students face. What are ways they can cope? Where can they go for help? Do Memory Photo Albums (page 22). Make Fact Pyramids (page 39).

2. Read and discuss pages 25–44. Have students discuss why Amelia wanted to go to school and the sacrifices she made to achieve her goal. Was schooling expensive in those days? Why is it important to get an education? Discuss the caption in the book beneath her senior picture: "The girl in brown who walks alone." Did this bother Amelia? Did she feel it was worth it to walk alone? Why? How did her first sight of an airplane affect her? Have students make a chart sequencing significant events in Amelia's flying education.

3. Discuss Amelia's notes to her parents while preparing for her *Friendship* flight. Describe Amelia's philosophy about life. Why did she write them these notes? How would her parents have felt if something had happened to Amelia on this flight? Have students do Coded Messages, page 43. Use Coast to Coast Flight, page 48, to help students understand the progressive development of airplanes. Have students write paragraphs comparing and contrasting Amelia's journey with one of today's modern airplanes.

Overview of Activities *(cont.)*

4. Read and discuss pages 45–65. Describe Amelia's first Atlantic to Pacific flight. What were some difficulties that occurred on her flights? How did these affect Amelia? How did Amelia plan for her flights? How did fame affect Amelia? Discuss her philosophy as expressed on pages 62–64. Have students do Character Webs (page 40).

5. Read and discuss pages 66–80. Discuss the preparation, difficulties, and dangers of this trip. Compare this information with the modern-day journey of the *Voyager*, page 38.

6. Read and discuss pages 81–90. Complete the sequence of events chart of Amelia's Last Flight (page 21). Discuss the difference between fact and opinion. Discuss what possibly happened to Amelia Earhart. Do Around the World map activity on page 60.

7. Read pages 91–99. Discuss the possibility of Amelia being captured by the Japanese.

8. Finish the book. Discuss the significance of Amelia's plane's name, the *Electra*. On a sheet of construction paper, have students glue down and color a picture of Amelia's plane and write a short explanation of its name next to it. (See Clip Art, page 75.)

Extending the Book

1. Research and discuss the effect of World War I and World War II on the development of the airplane. Invite a member of the Armed Forces to speak to your class about flying and the history of aviation in the military.

2. Research and discuss the effect of the airplane on travel, mail delivery, and world news. Ask the students to describe a world without air transportation.

3. Make books about how airplanes are used. (See pages 30–36.)

4. Collect news articles about women and men who are successful in their fields. Let students choose the area they would like to know more about and invite successful people in these fields to speak to the class. Have them write invitations and thank you letters.

5. Create a "Challenge and Courage Collage." Collect articles of people who are currently facing a challenge and displaying courage. Group the articles by the types of challenges. Are they physical, emotional, or mental challenges? How would students face them? Would they have the necessary courage? Use the articles to create a collage. Entitle it "Challenges and Courage." Display the collage in the classroom.

Amelia's Childhood

The Love of Reading

Amelia Earhart's family loved to read, and they frequently read aloud to one another. Amelia's father would often read to the family after dinner.

Make a list of five books you would recommend to your friends. Give a reason for your recommendation in the form of a teaser. A teaser is a brief caption which captures the attention of the reader. For example, *The Island of the Blue Dolphins* might have a teaser like: GIRL STRANDED! HER LIFE IS THREATENED! FIND OUT HOW SHE SURVIVES IN THIS SPELLBINDING ADVENTURE!

Books I Recommend

Book Name	Teaser
1.	
2.	
3.	
4.	
5.	

Setting Goals

Amelia's father had a great effect on her life. One important lesson she learned was to set goals and work hard to reach them.

Choose a realistic goal for this week, write it on an index card, and tape it to your desk. Set a goal that will take some extra effort for you to accomplish. Here are some ideas: Get 100% on all my spelling tests; read a book; learn about two countries in Europe; learn to play a new sport; help someone each day this week.

Last Flight

Read the pages of *Lost Star* that talk about Amelia's last flight. Then, fill in the sequence of events during that flight. Use complete sentences.

Time	What Happened
midnight	
12:30 a.m.	
1:15 a.m.	
1:30 a.m.	
2:45 a.m.	
3:00 a.m.	
3:15 a.m.	
3:30 a.m.	
3:45 a.m,	
5:00 a.m,	
6:15 a.m.	
6:45 a.m.	
7:42 a.m.	
7:58 a.m.	
8:45 a.m.	

Memory Photo Album

Amelia's life was filled with people and events of significance to her and others. What people and events are important in your life? Draw and label each in a photo frame below.

Bored—Nothing to Do!

by Peter Spier

Summary

Two bored boys have an idea and decide to build an airplane. They find all the parts they need from things around their house. Their plane actually flies! They have a wonderful adventure, but on returning to earth they face a family who is very unhappy with their solution to boredom.

The outline below is a suggested plan for using the various activities that are presented in this unit. You should adapt these ideas to fit your own classroom situation.

Sample Plan

Day 1

- Have students discuss and write about being bored.
- Student art: 5 dot activity (Setting the Stage, page 24)
- Student drawings and paragraphs (Enjoying the Book, page 24)
- Introduce Readers' Theater (pages 25–27)
- Art Activity—Mural (page 64)

Day 2

- Readers' Theater Rehearsal
- World's Busiest Airports (page 61)
- Math Activity: How Much Farther? (page 46)
- Character Web (page 40)

Day 3

- Reread the story
- Continue mural
- Readers' Theater rehearsal
- Daily Writing Topics (page 29)

Day 4

- Introduce Write Arounds (page 37)
- Continue Daily Writing Topics
- Readers' Theater dress rehearsal
- Math Activity—Distance Graph (page 47)

Day 5

- Make a Book (pages 30–36)
- Job Application (page 66)
- Present Readers' Theater
- Special Qualities (page 67)

Overview of Activities

Setting the Stage

1. Write "**BORED**" on the chalkboard, and brainstorm with the class things associated with this word. Focus on when and where students feel this way. Have students write one paragraph about what they would do if they could do anything they wanted to get rid of their boredom.

2. Give each student a paper with five large, black dots on it. Have students draw a picture incorporating the five dots. Students must not look at the papers of others for ideas. Share the drawings and discuss how each person sees things differently. For a similar activity, divide students into pairs. Have one student draw a squiggle line on a piece of paper, and have the second student draw a picture incorporating the line.

Enjoying the Book

1. Read the book aloud to the class without showing the pictures. Replace words that refer to flying (like airplane and landing) with your own nonsense words. Have each student draw a picture and write a paragraph about what he/she thinks the boys made. Reread the complete story and show the pictures. Discuss how students came up with their first impressions and how they felt after they realized the object was an airplane.

2. Introduce Readers' Theater with the class and begin rehearsals. (See pages 25–27.)

Extending the Book

1. The two boys in *Bored—Nothing To Do!* are very creative and inventive. Challenge your students to create or invent something that will be useful in the classroom. This can be done in small groups or as a homework assignment.

2. Introduce write arounds. (See page 37.) Model this activity by doing a story with the class. You add the first sentence to a prompt, then a student adds a second, you add the next, and so on, until you choose to end the story.

3. Have students make a mural for a backdrop to Readers' Theater. (See page 64 for ideas.)

4. Present Readers' Theater to parents, other classes, and the principal.

Readers' Theater

Readers' Theater is a style of performance done by players standing before an audience, using their voices only to create the characters and convey action. In order to perform Readers' Theater, students should understand its unique vocabulary. Review the list below with your students. Use these words when giving rehearsal directions.

Vocabulary

Script—copy of the play or story to be read

Rehearsal—practice of the play

Cast–people who are in the play

Player—what a person is called who is in a play

Understudy—another person who substitutes for a player

Upstage—toward the rear of the stage

Downstage—toward the front of the stage

Performance—the actual presentation of the play

Dress rehearsal—practice in costume exactly as it will be performed, last practice before the performance. (**Note:** costumes are not required in Readers' Theater; normal dress is acceptable.)

Bow—bending at the waist to thank the audience for their applause

Audience—people who watch the play

Offstage—any area that is not the stage

Applause/clapping—a gesture of gratitude

Rehearsal

Give each student two copies of the script (pages 26, 27). Have students place one copy inside a folded piece of 12" x 18" black construction paper. The other copy is to be left at home for practice. Have students highlight or underline their parts for the final performance. Have students (players) practice their parts sitting at their desks, standing at their desks, and finally, standing at the front of the classroom (stage).

Read the script with the class using the following suggestions:
1. Model reading—teacher reads only
2. Echo reading—teacher reads a line and students repeat it
3. Choral reading—teacher and class read together
4. Divide class into five groups and practice reading the script. (Teacher reads part 6.)
5. Divide your students in pairs and have them quietly read the script to one another by alternating lines.
6. Choose five students to read the script in front of the class.

The Performance

Assign groups or individual students to play each of the five parts. Have students line up offstage holding their scripts in folders in their upstage hand away from the audience. Have students walk on stage, turn and face the audience, and wait for the signal to raise and open their script folders. Have a student offstage read the opening credits and give a signal to start the performance. When the performance is finished, have students count silently from 1–4, then close and lower their folders with their upstage hands. Have students bow together and walk offstage. Choose new groups or individuals for a second performance.

Bored—Nothing to Do!

by Peter Spier (Adapted by Judy Vaden)

1: *Bored!*

2: *Two boys*

3: *Bored! Bored! Bored!*

All: *NOTHING TO DO!*

4: *Borrrrring!*

5: *Do something!*

6: *I was NEVER bored at your age!*

2: *I know! Let's make something.*

3: *What?*

1: *How?*

5: *HMMMM*

4: *Oh! I see! So that's how it works.*

3: *We're going to need LOTS of stuff!*

1: *Hammers and saws, wheels and wood and seats and*

2: *nails and paint and glue and*

4: *cloth and hinges and rope and*

5: *windshields and screws and motors and*

2: *LOTS of stuff*

1: *to build an airplane.*

3: *Swish swish bang bang rrrr rrrr*

1: *Hard work!!!*

2: *Bang bang zzzzz zzzzz swish swish*

3: *Need wire.*

4: *O.K. That's easy. This fence wire's perfect.*

5: *Engine. We need an engine!*

4: *Too little.*

2: *Too heavy.*

1: *Too old.*

3: *Just right!*

5: *Oooo!*

2: *Aaaah!*

3: *Uuuh!*

1: *Messy!*

4: *Tiring!*

5: *Well done!*

1: *Turn the key.*

5: *Sputter…splatte…rrrrrr*

2: *Up, up, up*

3: *Noisy!*

4: *IT WORKS!*

1: *IT FLIES!*

5: *IT REALLY, REALLY FLIES!*

2: *WOW!*

1: *GREAT PLANE!*

2: *SOARING!*

3: *SWOOPING!*

4: *GLIDING!*

5: *Grumble, grumble, grumble*

2: *TV doesn't work. Call a repairman.*

4: *Phone doesn't work. Call a repairman.*

1: *Car doesn't start.*

3: *WHAAAT!!!*

Bored—Nothing to Do! *(cont.)*

4: *Where are the sheets?*

5: *the clothesline? the carriage wheels?*

2: *What happened to the fence?*

5: *the bicycles? the garden furniture?*

3: *NOTHING WORKS!*

1: *WHERE ARE THE BOYS?*

2: *Come down NOW!*

4: *Uh-oh. They're angry.*

5: *Better go down.*

4: *Perfect landing.*

3: *Put it all back!*

2: *The engine, the windshield, . . .*

1: *the wheels, the wire, the fence, . . .*

3: *the tools? the paint?*

4: *Go to your room!*

5: *Clever boys.*

2: *Bored!*

3: *Two boys*

1: *Bored! Bored! Bored! All: NOTHING TO DO!*

1: *HMMMMMMMMMM.*

2: *I have an idea!! (Cast forms a circle and whispers to each other.)*

All: *Let's pst...pst...pst...pst (Cast faces audience.)*

All: *YEAH!*

Daily Writing Topics

For *"Orville Wright and Wilbur Wright"*

1. Write a letter to the Smithsonian Institution, the National Oceanic and Atmospheric Administration (U.S. Weather Bureau), or NASA requesting information on a topic. Give a 2 minute oral report on the information you received. Here are the addresses:

   Smithsonian Institution　　　**National Oceanic and Atmospheric Administration**
   1000 Jefferson Dr. S.W.　　　　U.S. Department of Commerce
   Washington, D.C. 20560　　　　Washington, D.C. 20230

   　　　　　　　NASA
   　　　　　　　Kennedy Space Center
   　　　　　　　Florida 32809

2. Write a paragraph on how you think the Wright brothers felt when they discovered that Otto Lilienthal's flight calculations were wrong. What lesson did they learn?

3. Pretend you are Wilbur Wright and write a letter to your father describing your progress at Kitty Hawk, South Carolina.

4. Pretend to be Orville Wright and write a one-page autobiography.

5. Write a news article entitled, "The First Flight."

6. Write an editorial in which you give the opinion that flying is useless.

7. Write an editorial predicting that the airplane will be the greatest human invention and describe its effect on the world.

For *The Glorious Flight*

1. Write an advertisement announcing the contest to fly across the English Channel.

2. Pretend to be Blériot and keep a journal including your flight attempts, failures, and airplane designs. Describe how you felt when you finally had success.

3. Write a newspaper article declaring the winner of the contest.

4. Use the Venn diagram from page 16 to write paragraphs comparing and contrasting the flights of Blériot and Charles Lindbergh. (See their biographies on pages 13 and 15.)

5. Write a paragraph describing the differences between the first and last airplane designs and flights of Louis Blériot.

Daily Writing Topics *(cont.)*

For *Lost Star*

1. Describe how Amelia's mother was different from many mothers and how she influenced Amelia.

2. Describe Amelia's childhood adventures.

3. Amelia's senior class picture had the caption: "The girl in brown who walks alone." How did this make Amelia feel? Write about two examples from Amelia's life that show this caption to be true or false.

4. Describe the steps Amelia took to become a pilot.

5. In 1928 Amelia was hired to write for the magazine, *Cosmopolitan*. She wrote many articles about flying. Some titles were: "Try Flying Yourself," "Is it Safe to Fly?," and "Why are Women Afraid to Fly?" Choose one of these titles and write an article pretending to be Amelia.

6. Write an editorial giving reasons why women should not be allowed to fly.

7. Write an article convincing people that space flight will be a safe way to travel.

8. Amelia's plane was named after the constellation, *Electra*. Is there any significance in relation to Amelia's last flight?

9. Describe the planning and preparation needed for an around-the-world flight.

10. Write a news article describing Amelia's take-off for her around-the-world flight.

11. Write a news article summarizing her around-the-world flight.

12. At each stop on her flight around-the-world, Amelia mailed a letter to her husband. Write a letter at these stops like Amelia did. Include how Amelia felt about her successes and the obstacles she encountered each day.

13. Write a news article about Amelia's disappearance.

14. Write an article describing what you think happened to Amelia Earhart. Use supporting evidence.

For *Bored—Nothing to Do!*

1. Write a story about something you could make from objects in your home.

2. Write a story describing where you would fly if you could go anywhere in the world. Why would you fly to that place?

3. Write about three things you like to do when you are bored.

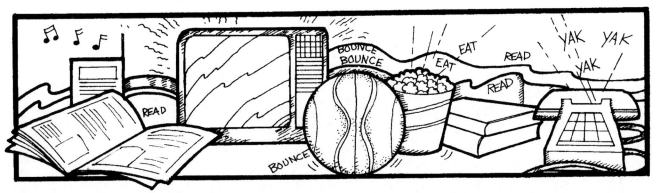

Book Ideas

Have students work individually or in groups to write books using the ideas below. Listed next to each topic are suggested book-making methods. (See pages 31–36 for book-making directions.)

1. **Unusual Planes** (All methods)
   On each page, have students draw one of the planes listed below and write its name or a sentence describing it. (See Clip Art, pages 75–78.)

   Hawker Siddeley Harrier: airplane that takes off and lands like a helicopter.

   Concorde: supersonic transport plane. Its first flight was in 1969. It can carry 100 passengers, and can fly at Mach 2 (twice the speed of sound). The *Concorde* is 204 feet long. The heat outside is so great during the flight that the aluminum plane stretches 10 inches. It has a special design to withstand the sonic boom shock wave when it passes through the sound barrier.

   Lockheed C-5 Galaxy: has hinged nose that opens to load 132 tons of cargo. It is used for long range transport and is one of the largest airplanes flying today.

   Helicopters: Aircraft which take-off and land vertically. Rotor blades on top of helicopters spin very fast and pull down air which pushes against the ground and lifts the helicopter off the ground.

   Spruce Goose: 219-foot airplane with eight propeller engines built by Howard Hughes. It has the longest wingspan of any plane ever built—320 feet! It was flown only once in a test flight.

2. **Useful Planes** (All methods)
   Have students use encyclopedias, airplane books, and clip art (pages 75–78) to create a book for several types of airplanes. On each page, have students draw a picture of each plane and write its name or a sentence describing it. Here are some suggestions: passenger, freight, recreation, mail, highway patrol, crop duster, forest management, fire fighter, map maker, hurricane hunter, Strategic Air Command, reconnaissance.

3. **Occupations in the Airplane Industry** (Big Book, Wheel, Pop-Up)
   On each page, have students draw a picture of a person on the job and write a job title or a short explanation beneath it. (See Flight Careers, page 65.)

4. **Parts of an Airplane** (Wheel, Pop-Up)
   Have students draw pictures of each airplane part and beneath it write the name of the part or a sentence about what the part does. (See Airplane Parts, page 44.)

5. **Lindbergh's Famous Flight** (Big Book, Wheel)
   Have students write a creative story about Lindbergh's Atlantic crossing using an encyclopedia and the biography on page 15.

6. **People Who Influenced the Development of Flight** (Wheel, Pop-Up)
   On each page have students illustrate a famous person's contribution to the development of flight and write the person's name beneath it. (See Milestones, page 58)

Making Books

When students have completed the inside pages of their books, have them make the pages below. Have students look at other books for creative ideas.

Parts of a Book

1. **Front Cover:** includes book title, author's name, illustration, and illustrator's name. (Example: *Useful Planes* by Room 5, Period 4.)

2. **Title Page:** Includes book title, author and illustrator, and publishing company.

3. **Dedication Page:** honors one or more special people.

4. **Table of Contents:** lists what is inside the book by subject or by authors.

5. **Author Page:** describes the author. This page can include the author's family background, hobbies, and other books written by the author.

6. **Back Cover:** may include an illustration and book reviews from magazines, book clubs, newspapers, etc.

On this page and the next, there are several book-making methods. Select one appropriate for your book topic.

Big Books

Purchase blank big books at teacher supply stores or make your own.

Materials: Tagboard or heavy paper; metal rings; hole punch; hole reinforcers; crayons, colored pencils or markers; scissors; glue

Directions: Have students make book pages from sheets of tagboard. Punch three holes on the left hand side of each sheet of tagboard. Cover the front and back of each hole with hole reinforcers. Connect all pages with metal rings.

Making Books *(cont.)*

Shape Books

Materials: Construction paper, tagboard, or heavy paper; crayons, colored pencils or markers; pencil; scissors; stapler

Directions:

Have students trace enough copies of the airplane pattern shape on page 33 to use as book pages. Provide each student with a copy of the pattern as is for the cover. Have students write sentences and do illustrations on each page. Combine the finished pages and staple them together along one edge.

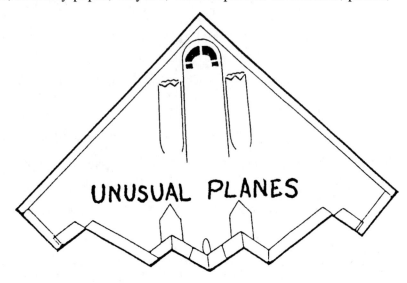

Wheel Books

Materials: Construction paper or tagboard; scissors; crayons or colored pencils; brads; pencil

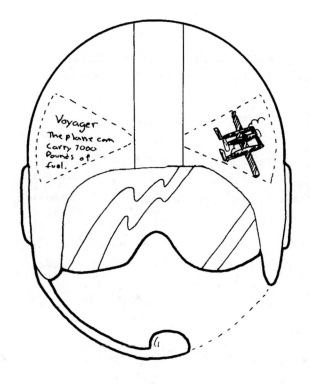

Directions:

Make copies of the patterns on pages 34 and 35. Have students cut out the wheel pattern, the flight helmet and the dashed windows on the flight helmet. Help students attach the center of the wheel behind the flight helmet with a brad. Direct students to color their helmets. Have students draw a picture in the wheel section on the right side of the helmet. In the wheel section, on the left side of the helmet, have students write a sentence or a word describing the picture. Help students turn their wheels and repeat this procedure until all wheel sections are completed. (There should be four written sections and four picture sections.)

Shape Book Pattern

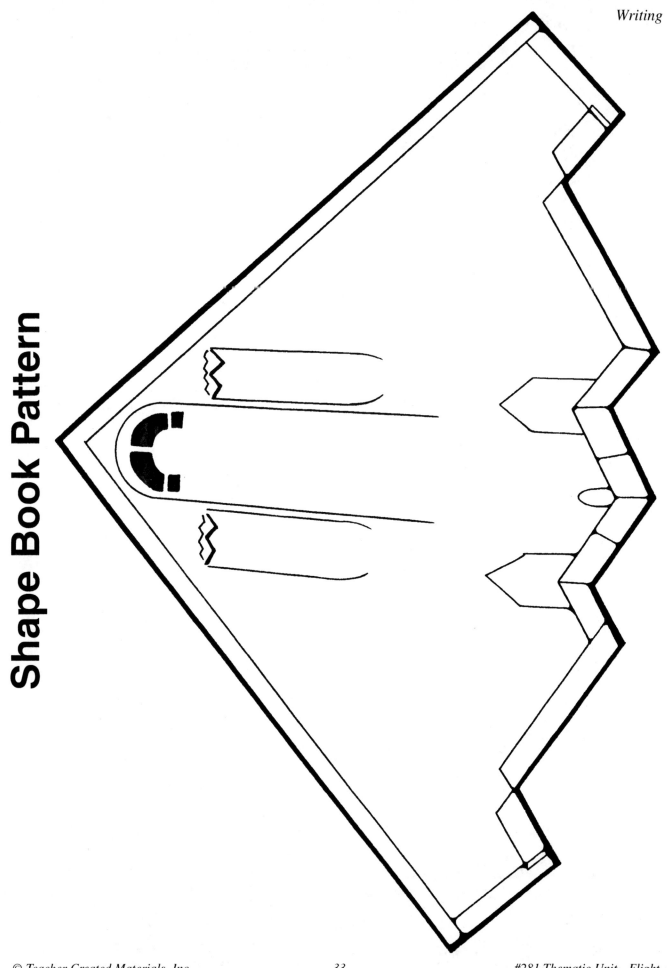

Wheel Book Pattern

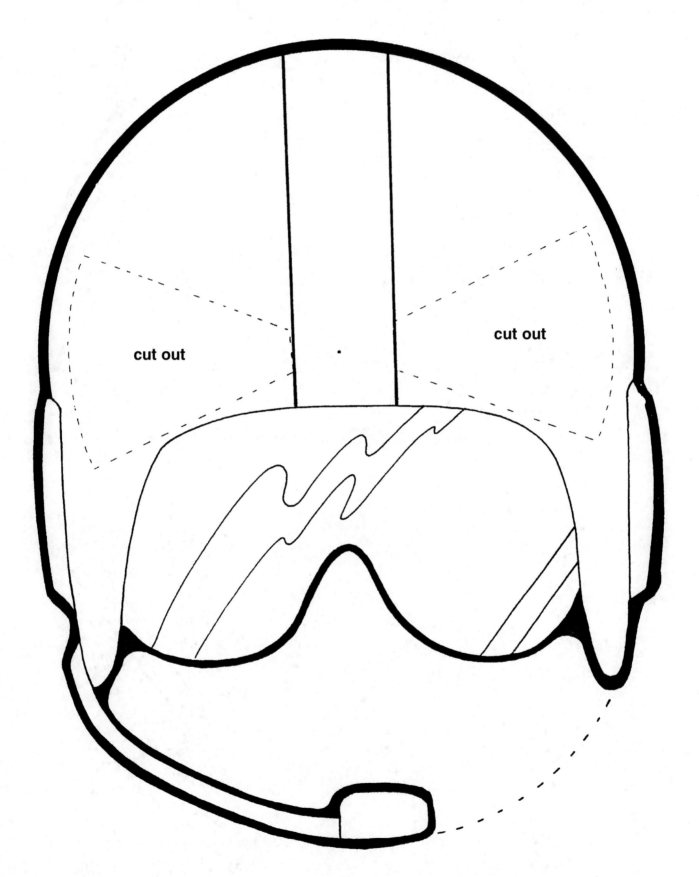

cut out

cut out

Wheel Book Pattern *(cont.)*

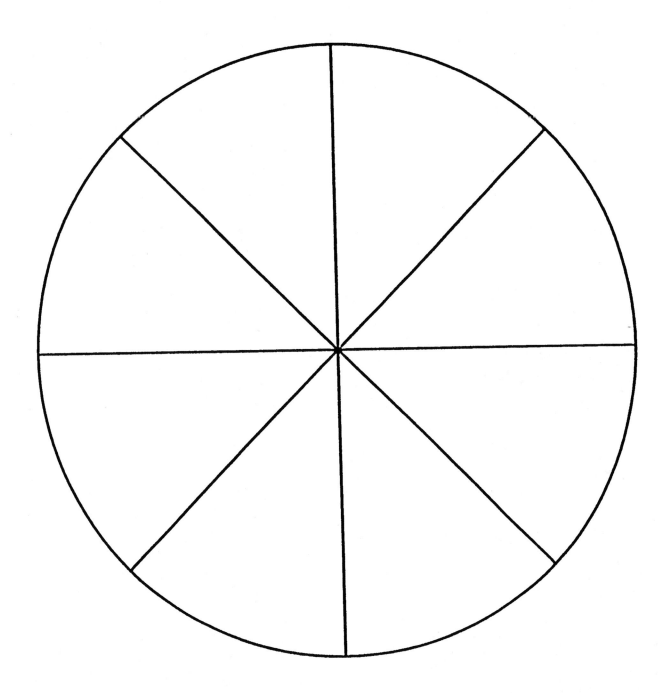

Making Books *(cont.)*

Pop-Up Books

Materials: White construction paper; crayons, colored pencils or markers; glue; scissors

Directions

1. Have students fold a piece of construction paper in half and cut slits ½ down from the fold.

2. Help students push the cut area through the fold and crease it to form the pop-up section.

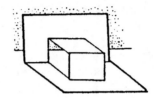

3. Have students make other pop-up pages and glue them back to back.

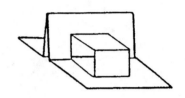

4. Help students write sentences above the pop-up section and glue an appropriate picture from a magazine or a drawing to the pop-up page.

5. Help students glue a cover to their pop-up books.

Pop-Up Index Cards

Have students write a flight question on the index card cover, and write and illustrate the answer on the pop-up section inside.

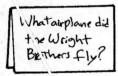

Multiple Pop-Ups

Have students make several pop-up sections on each page.

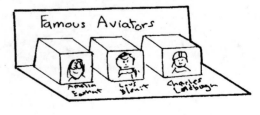

Write Around

A write around is a writing activity in which students collectively write a story by each contributing one sentence.

Method 1

Write a prompt on the board. (See prompts below.) Explain to students that the sentences they make up must make sense with the prompt.

Have one student add a sentence to the prompt.

Have another student add a second sentence.

Continue this procedure until students complete the story.

Method 2

Divide the class into circles of five students, and give each student a sheet of paper. Explain that there is no talking and that spelling is not important. Ideas are what count.

Have students write down the prompt and a response sentence on their papers.

After one minute, have students pass their papers to the student to their left and write a third sentence on the paper now in front of them. Have students continue to pass their papers until they have their own papers in front of them again.

Have students in each group read their stories quietly to one another, and choose two to read to the class.

Help the class write a list of positive comments to critique the stories. ("I liked the description of, . . ." "The action was excellent in . . .," "The characters were fascinating in . . .," etc.)

Have the class vote on their favorite story.

Prompts

Wilbur and Orville Wright were delighted after their first flight. Now they could turn their attention to their next project.

After Louis Blériot flew across the English Channel, he decided to...

Airplanes searched for Amelia Earhart for days, but finally, the search was suspended. Five years later, a letter in a bottle was found on a busy beach.

The two boys had finished building their airplane. They looked at each other and . . .

Voyager

The Wright brothers, Amelia Earhart, Louis Blériot, and Charles Lindbergh all set world records for airplane flying. Today, modern records are still being set. The flight of the *Voyager* is one example. Read the paragraph and answer the questions below.

On December 14, 1986, a unique plane called the *Voyager* took off from Edwards Air Force base in California. It was going on a long, non-stop flight around the world. The *Voyager* was a special plane because it was made of paper honey comb and weighed less than 2000 pounds. It had taken six years for a man named Burt Rutan to design and construct this non-metal plane. The *Voyager* had 17 fuel tanks for the long journey. The plane could carry a supply of 7000 pounds of fuel because it was so lightweight.

During the trip, the *Voyager* flew at an average speed of 116 miles per hour. The pilots, Dick Rutan and Jeana Yeager, took along dried food that did not need to be refrigerated like energy bars, fruit, and crackers. They carried 20 gallons of water in a collapsible container. For emergencies, they took a supply of bottled oxygen. During the trip, the *Voyager* flew 25,012 miles. The journey took 9 days, 3 minutes, and 44 seconds. The *Voyager* landed on December 23, 1986 back in California to complete its historic flight.

List four things which describe the *Voyager* **airplane**.

1. _____   3. _____

2. _____   4. _____

List four **supplies** the pilots took on their journey.

1. _____   3. _____

2. _____   4. _____

List four things describing the **flight** of the *Voyager*.

1. _____

3. _____

Why was the *Voyager* made of paper instead of metal?

_____

_____

The Fact Pyramid

Write the name of an aviator on the bottom of the pyramid (the square in the center below). Write one fact about them on each of the triangular sides. Cut out the pattern, fold on the dotted lines, and tape or glue the edges together. Memorize one fact each day. Make a different Fact Pyramid for Amelia Earhart, Louis Blériot and the Wright brothers. Read only the facts to your classmates, and have them guess the pilot.

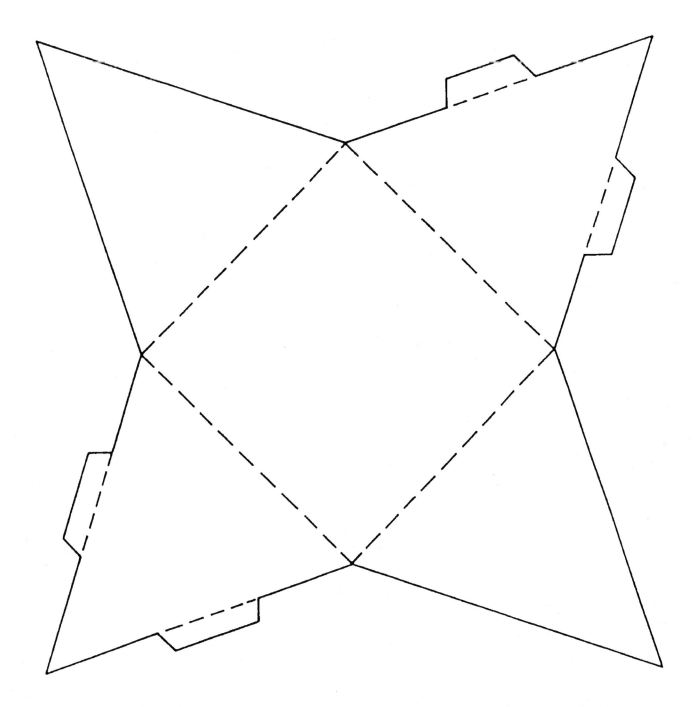

Character Web for

_____

(name of person)

1. **Draw and/or name a famous person who influenced the development of flight in the center circle. For ideas, see Milestones, page 58.**

2. **Write a character quality in each rectangle. (See list to right.)**

3. **In the ovals, write the examples of things this person did or said which reflect their character traits.**

QUALITIES

resourceful–truthful–trustworthy–
courageous–independent–determined–inquisitive–
patient–dependable–persistent–carin–respectful–
fair–responsible–edicated–honest–vision–
creative–ingenuity–brave–adventurous

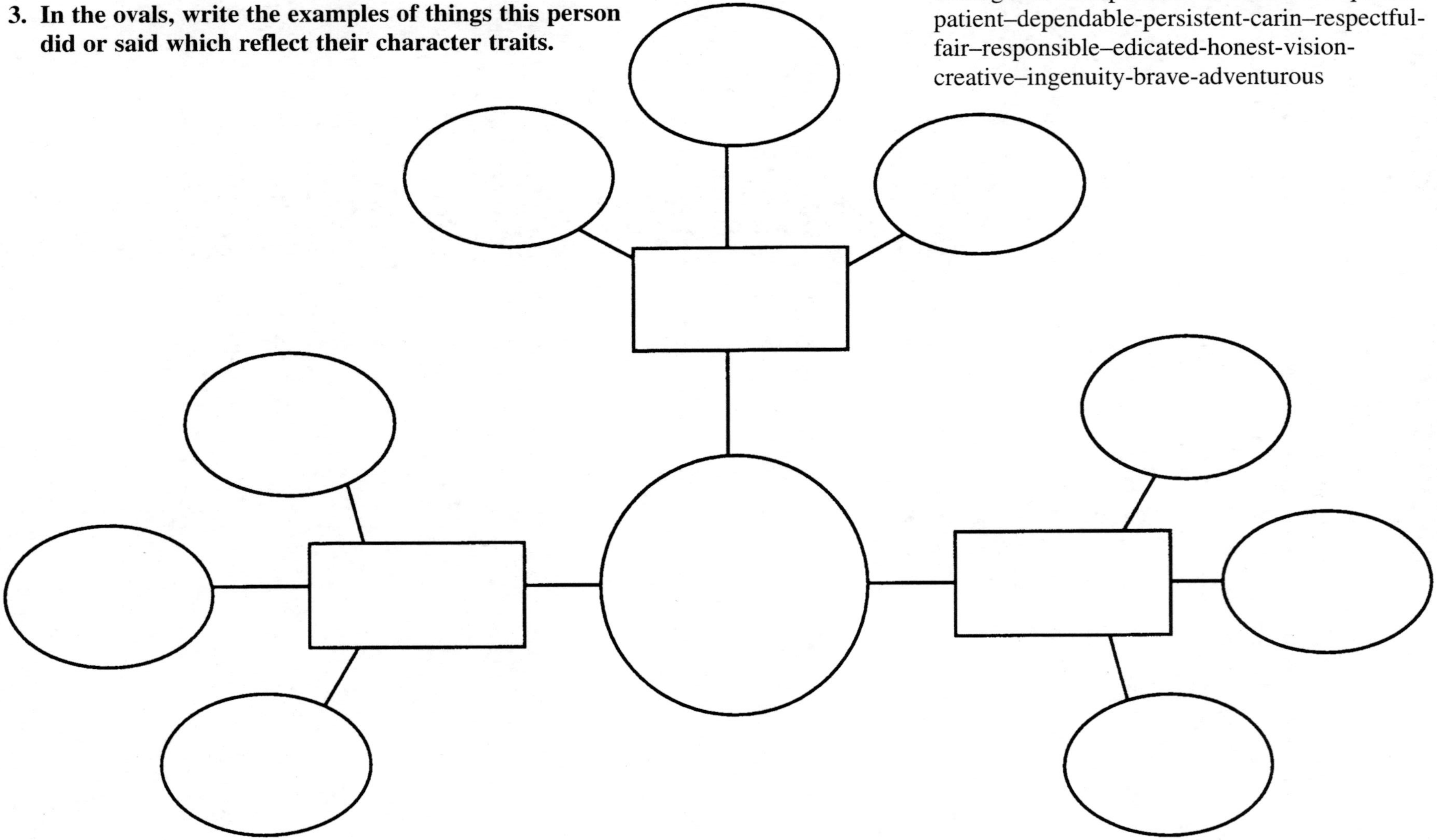

Vocabulary Activities

Group Dictionary Work: Divide the class into groups of 5 or 6. Discuss the importance of cooperating with each other in groups. Talk about the concepts of job-sharing, division of labor, and assembly line production. Assign a set of vocabulary words for each group to look up in the dictionary (see Word Bank, page 42). Have students discuss how they are going to complete the assignment as a group. Have each group turn in one sheet of paper with the following items: vocabulary words and their definitions, dictionary page numbers for each word, and the guide words from the top of the dictionary page where each vocabulary word was found. To liven up the activity, have groups compete to see who completes the activity first.

3" x 5" Cards: Write each vocabulary word on a 3" x 5" card and its definition on a separate 3" x 5" card. Use the cards for the activities suggested below or others of your choice.

Alphabet Line-ups: Pass out only the vocabulary word cards to students. Tell students to put the cards in alphabetical order by lining up in front of the classroom. Allow students to help each other if they whisper. After the class has lined up, have the first student in line say the word on his/her card. Have the class repeat the word. Continue down the line with the same procedure. Have students raise their hands if they think the order is incorrect. Have the class decide on the correct order. After the words are in correct order, collect them and repeat the activity with the same words at least 3 times. To enhance the alphabet line-up, have students try to give definitions for each word.

Partners: Mix up all vocabulary word and definition cards. Give one card to each student. Have students find their partners with the proper match. Tell students to whisper. Have partners stand together in front of the class. After everyone is matched, have each pair read their word and its definition or have the class guess its definition. Have students raise their hands if they think the vocabulary word is matched incorrectly with its definition. Have students decide the correct definition. After words are matched correctly, collect all cards and repeat the activity at least 3 times.

Pictionary: Divide the class into teams of 4 or 5 and use word cards only. Have a student select a vocabulary word from the pile, and illustrate the word on the board. The first team to say the word gets a point.

Categories: Pass out word cards only to students. Have students group the words into categories by standing in different parts of the room. Allow students to whisper to each other. Categories might include: airplane parts, kinds of aircraft, flight occupations, etc.

Vocabulary Pictures: Have students draw pictures using the vocabulary words as picture lines.

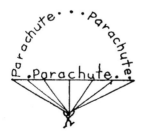 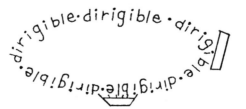 

Examples:

Picture Dictionary: Have students write and illustrate vocabulary words and their definitions on sheets of construction paper. Bind the pages into a big book. (See page 31.)

Word Bank

AIRCRAFT

glider	autogiro	tanker	crop duster	passenger
blimp	monoplane	bomber	triplane	experimental
dirigible	sailplane	fighter	fire plane	*Air Force One*
amphibian	seaplane	reconnaissance	mapmaker	trainer
ornithopter	helicopter	biplane	highway patrol	electronic
airship	transport	stunt plane	cargo plane	search and rescue

AIRPLANE PARTS

rudder	tachometer	fuselage	wing tip	fin
wing	gauge	landing gear	fuel tank	transmitter
jet	anemometer	stick	air intake	instrument
propeller	airfoil	trailing edge	cabin	panel
cockpit	throttle	leading edge	landing lights	parachute
aileron	elevator	windshield	cabin door	nacelle
altimeter	flaps	taillight	jet pod	cowling

FLIGHT TERMS

solo	landing	revolutions	visibility	jet thrust
aviation	take-off	rotate	hangar	wing span
navigator	visibility	atmosphere	FAA	soar
pilot	altitude	ceiling	flight pattern	taxi
mechanic	attitude	environment	aerodynamics	autopilot
aerodynamics	monsoon	headwind	banking	compass
meteorologist	aloft	VTOL	supersonic	

Coded Messages

It is important for airplane pilots to communicate clearly. A standard code was developed which is used by all pilots and airline personnel. Each letter of the alphabet is assigned a word. When a word is spelled over the airwaves, it is spelled with words, not letters.(Example: **WING:** **W**hiskey, **I**ndian, **N**ovember, **G**olf)

Write the words below in code using the standard code on this page.

A _____   W _____

I _____   E _____

R _____   A _____

P _____   T _____

L _____   H _____

A _____   E _____

N _____   R _____

E _____

(Your name)

P _____   — _____

I _____   — _____

L _____   — _____

O _____   — _____

T _____   — _____

                          — _____

J _____   — _____

E _____   — _____

T _____   — _____

A	**Alfa**
B	**Bravo**
C	**Charlie**
D	**Delta**
E	**Echo**
F	**Foxtrot**
G	**Golf**
H	**Hotel**
I	**India**
J	**Juliet**
K	**Kilo**
L	**Lima**
M	**Mike**
N	**November**
O	**Oscar**
P	**Papa**
Q	**Quebec**
R	**Romeo**
S	**Sierra**
T	**Tango**
U	**Uniform**
V	**Victor**
W	**Whiskey**
X	**X-Ray**
Y	**Yankee**
Z	**Zulu**

Airplane Parts

Identify the parts using the list of words below.

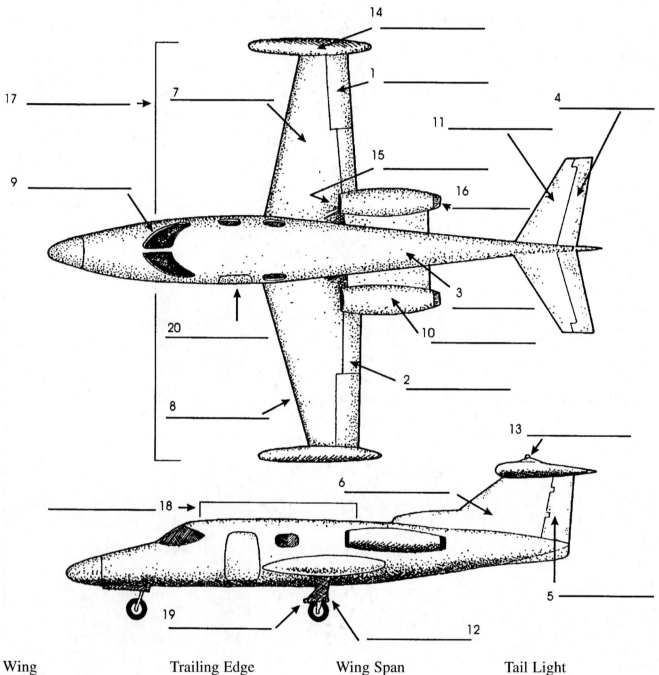

Wing	Trailing Edge	Wing Span	Tail Light
Leading Edge	Fuselage	Cabin	Wing-Tip Fuel Tank
Windshield	Elevators	Landing Light	Air Intake
Jet Pod	Rudder	Cabin Door	Jet Thrust
Horizontal Stabilizer	Fin	Landing Gear	Ailerons

Airplane Measurement

This exercise helps students see the relative lengths of different types of aircraft.

Materials: 1500 ft. (455 meters) of twine; scissors; yardsticks or rulers; stapler; 3" x 5" cards

Directions:
- Have students cut twine into the lengths shown below.
- Have students in pairs stretch the airplane lengths out across a field.
- Staple a 3" x 5" card with the name of the airplane to the appropriate length of twine.
- Have students measure their bodies, their bedrooms, their parents' cars, or the outside of their homes with twine, and compare these lengths with the lengths of the planes the following day.
- Copy the chart and questions below for your students.

AIRPLANE	LENGTH feet	meters
Boeing 737	119	36.1
Boeing 707	153	46.4
DC Super 61	187	56.7
DC-9	120	36.4
Boeing 747	231	70
Concorde	193	58.5
Spruce Goose	219	66.4
Wright brothers' Flyer	21	6.4
Voyager	33	10

Use the chart above to answer these questions.

1. How many meters longer is the *Spruce Goose* than the Concorde? _____ meters
2. What is the total length in meters of the *Voyager*, 747, and DC-9? _____ meters
3. How many feet longer is the *Spruce Goose* than the Wright brothers' *Flyer*? _____ feet
4. What is the total length in feet of all the Boeing airplanes? _____ feet
5. How many feet is 70 meters? _____ feet
6. How many meters is 153 feet? _____ meters

How Much Farther?

The Wright brothers' airplane flew at a speed of 30 miles per hour. At this speed, their plane could fly a distance of 30 miles in one hour. In two hours they could fly 60 miles. Complete the distance charts for each of the following planes.

Wright brothers' *Flyer*: (30 mph)

Hours Flying	Distance (miles)
1	30
2	60
3	
4	
5	

Boeing 747: (625 mph)

Hours Flying	Distance (miles)
1	625
2	
3	
4	
5	

Blériot Xl: (38 mph)

Hours Flying	Distance (miles)
1	38
2	
3	
4	
5	

Concorde: (1550 mph)

Hours Flying	Distance (miles)
1	1,550
2	
3	
4	
5	

Amelia Earhart's *Electra*: (70 mph)

Hours Flying	Distance (miles)
1	70
2	
3	
4	
5	

Space Shuttle: (16,000 mph)

Hours Flying	Distance (miles)
1	16,000
2	
3	
4	
5	

Distance Graph

Make a bar graph to show how far each plane can travel in **one** hour. Use the information from page 46.

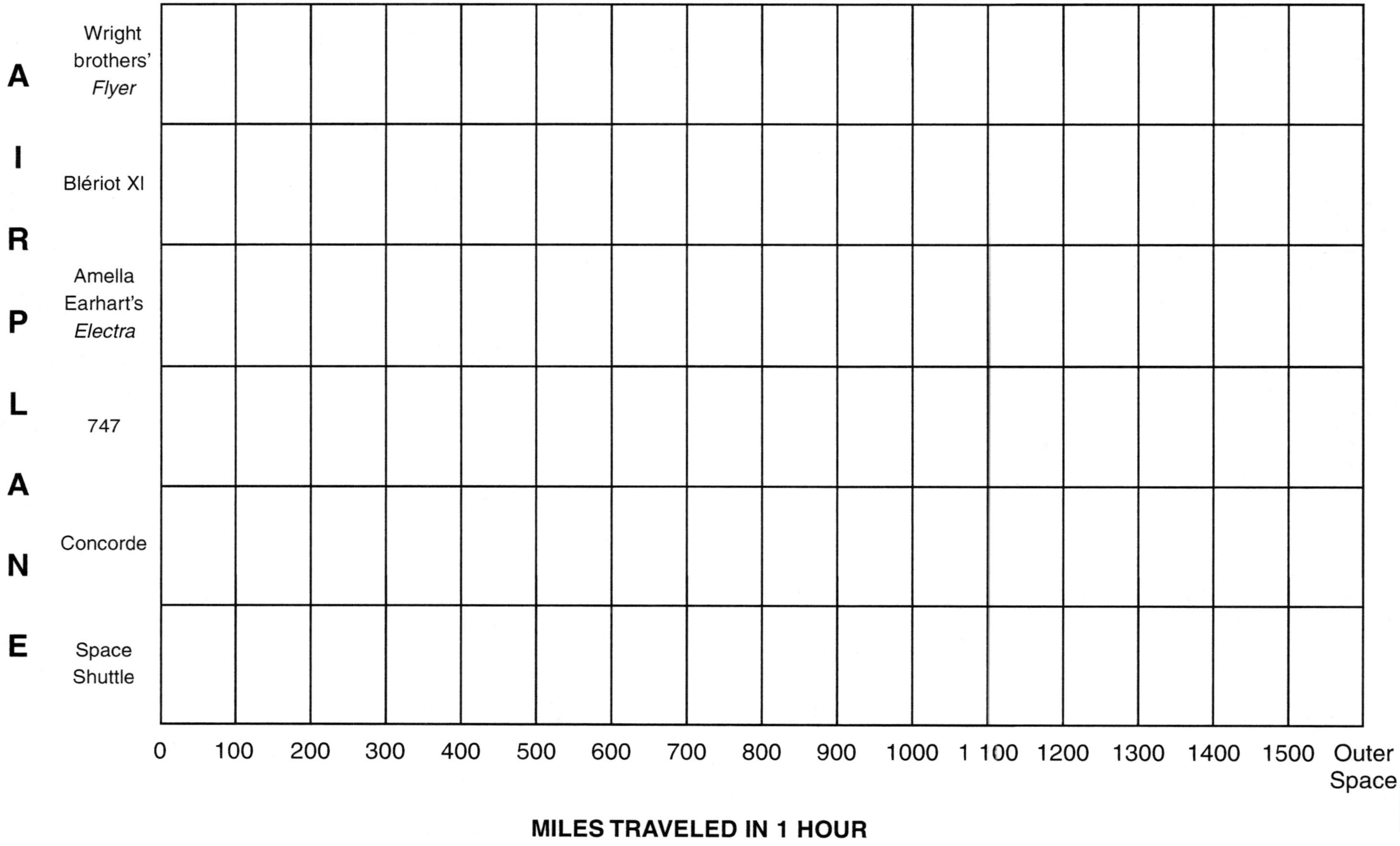

Math

Outer
Space

	0	100	200	300	400	500	600	700	800	900	1000	1100	1200	1300	1400	1500	
A	Wright brothers' *Flyer*																
I	Blériot XI																
R	Amelia Earhart's *Electra*																
P	747																
L																	
A	Concorde																
N																	
E	Space Shuttle																

MILES TRAVELED IN 1 HOUR

Math

Coast to Coast

As airplanes improved over the years, they were built to fly faster and faster. Traveling by plane from New York to Los Angeles, a distance of 2700 miles, took less and less time.

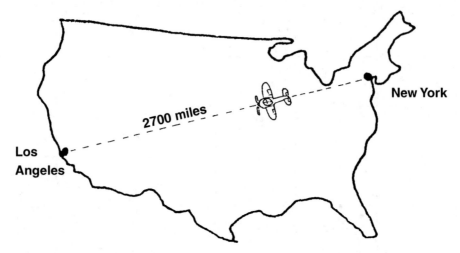

When you know the distance a vehicle travels and the rate (or speed) at which it travels, you can calculate the time it will take to make the trip. Mathematicians use this formula, $\frac{d}{r} = t$, which stands for: distance ÷ rate = time. For example, if you know that a plane flies at the rate of 90 miles per hour (mph), you can discover its flying time from New York to Los Angeles by doing the following division:

$$\frac{2700 \text{ miles}}{90 \text{ mph}} = 30 \text{ hours}$$

Use the formula and a calculator to complete the chart below to show how long it would take each of these famous planes to fly from New York to Los Angeles.

Year	Plane	Distance (N.Y. to L.A.)	Rate (Speed in m.p.h.)	Flying Time (rounded to nearest hour)
1903	Wright brothers' *Flyer*	2700	30	_____ hours
1909	*Blériot XI*	2700	38	_____ hours
1922	Amelia's Earhart's First Plane	2700	70	_____ hours
1970	Boeing 747	2700	625	_____ hours
1976	Concorde	2700	1550	_____ hours

Extensions: Determine how long it would take to drive from New York to Los Angeles if your average speed was 50 mph.

Find the distances between other pairs of cities and calculate how long it would take the planes on the chart to fly between them.

48 © *Teacher Created Materials, Inc.*

Flying High

The things in the columns below all fly at different heights.
Complete the chart using the formulas below.
Use a calculator if necessary.

FEET ÷ 5280 = MILES

MILES x 5280 = FEET

MILES x 1.6 = KILOMETERS

KILOMETERS x 1000 = METERS

Name	Feet	Miles	Kilometers	Meters
Jet		7		
Helicopter	42,240			
Cirrus Clouds		4		
Whistling Swan		1		
Verreaux Eagle	5280			
Space Shuttle		170		
Unmanned Balloon		27		
Two-Passenger Plane	15,840			

1. Which object flies highest? _____

2. Which object flies lowest? _____

3. How much higher does the helicopter fly than a two-passenger plane? _____ feet

4. What two objects fly at the same altitude? _____ _____

5. How high does the Space Shuttle fly? _____ miles

Altitude Records

As the science of aviation has developed, planes have been able to fly higher and higher. This chart shows some of the altitude records that have been set over the years.

Aviator	Country	Year	Record Altitude	
			In Feet	In Meters
O. Wright	U,S.	1909	1,637	499
G. Legagneux	France	1913	20,079	6,120
W. Neuenhofen	Germany	1929	41,795	12,739
M. Pezzi	Italy	1938	56,046	17,083
J. Cunningham	Great Britain	1948	59,445	18,119
H. C. Johnson	U.S.	1958	91,243	27,811
J. A, Walker	U.S.	1962	246,750	75,209
J. A. Walker	U.S.	1963	354,200	107,960

Complete the bar graph below to show these altitudes graphically.

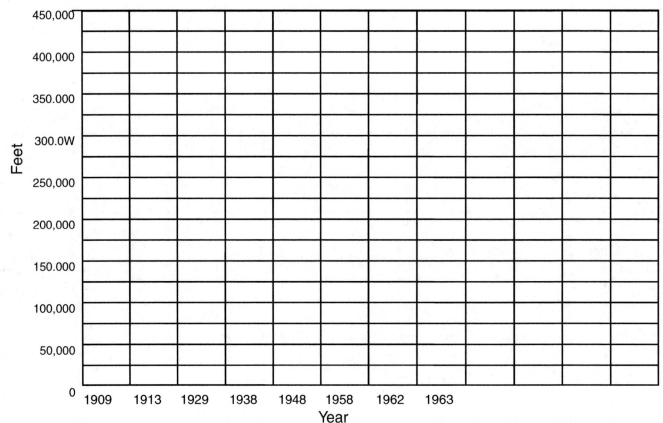

Extensions: Find additional records to add to the chart. Make a graph to show the records in meters.

Find Your Weight!

Space flight allows mankind to escape the earth's gravity. Because the gravity of other heavenly bodies varies, your weight would be different from your weight on the earth. Complete the chart using the formula below to find your weight on the planets and sun. Use a calculator if necessary. Round decimal answers to nearest hundredth.

YOUR WEIGHT x DECIMAL = YOUR WEIGHT ON ANOTHER PLANET
To change pounds to kilograms, multiply by .45
To change kilograms to pounds, multiply by 2.2

Planet	Decimal	Your Weight (pounds)	(kilograms)
Earth	1.00		
Moon	0.17		
Mercury	0.38		
Venus	0.88		
Mars	39		
Jupiter	2.65		
Saturn	1.17		
Uranus	1.05		
Neptune	1.06		
Pluto	0.25		
Sun	26.00		

1. Where do you weigh the most? _____

2. On what planet do you weigh the least? _____

3. How much do you weigh on the moon? _____

4. How much do you weigh on Mars _____

Scientific Method

A scientist is someone who asks many questions and tries to learn the answers by doing experiments. He/she follows a procedure which is a step-by-step way of doing things. First, a scientist finds a question that needs to be answered. Next, a scientist does research. He/she investigates and gathers facts about a subject. Then the scientist develops a hypothesis which is an explanation of what he/she thinks will happen. A scientist then tests the hypothesis by doing an experiment. An experiment is a way to test what happens to something. The scientist collects data or information by observing, measuring, and carefully recording the results or outcome of the experiment.

Then a scientist draws a conclusion or final decision about what happened by examining the data. A conclusion explains why something happens. Finally, a scientist writes a report about the findings so that others can learn from the experiments. This orderly method of research is called the scientific method.

Use the information from the paragraph above to write your own definitions for the following words:

1. Scientist:_____

2. Experiment: _____

3. Research: _____

4. Data:_____

5. Scientific Method: _____

6. Hypothesis: _____

7. Procedure: _____

8. Results:_____

9. Conclusion: _____

Experiment Form

Question

_____

_____

_____

Hypothesis

_____

_____

Procedure

Materials: _____

Directions: _____

_____

_____

_____

_____

_____

_____

Results

_____

_____

Conclusion

_____

_____

Science Experiments

For all experiments, follow the rules of a good scientist. Complete the Experiment Form on page 53 for each experiment. Do your best to explain WHY things happen in your experiment. Be ready to report your findings to the class.

Lift

Lift is the force that pushes up on an airplane and gives it the ability to climb into the air and stay up during flight. More than 250 years ago, Daniel Bernoulli, a Swiss scientist, observed in experiments that when air flows over a surface of an object the force pushing down on that surface is reduced, and the force pushing up on the surface becomes greater. This causes the object to lift off the ground. Try your own lift experiments from the ideas below.

1. What will happen to the strip of paper?

Materials: 2" x 10" paper strip

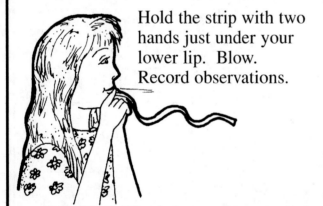

Hold the strip with two hands just under your lower lip. Blow. Record observations.

2. What will happen to the 3" x 5" card?

Materials: 3" x 5" card, funnel

Hold the funnel with the large end down over the card. Suck air through the funnel. Record observations. Blow air through the funnel. Record observations.

3. What will happen to the stamp?

Materials: one stamp, one quarter

Lay the stamp on your desk. Hold the quarter 1" over the stamp and blow down on the coin. Record observations.

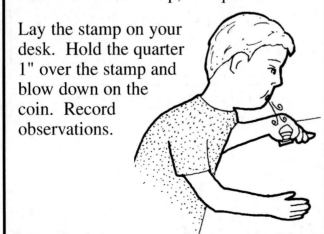

4. Can you pick up the paper?

Materials: pencil, paper cup, sheet of paper

Put the paper on the desk. Use the other objects to pick up the paper without touching the paper with your hands. Record observations.

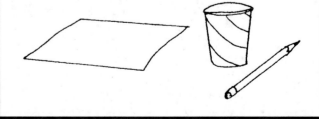

Science Experiments *(cont.)*

Gravity

Gravity is a natural force of the earth that pulls down on an airplane. For an airplane to fly, the upward force of lift must be greater than the downward force of gravity. All objects stay on the ground because of gravity. The greater the force of gravity on an object, the more it weighs. The famous astronomer, Galileo, studied gravity and how it affected falling objects. Try the gravity experiments below to find out for yourself, how gravity works.

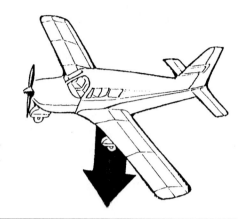

1. Do heavy objects fall faster than lighter ones?

Materials: different objects: pencil, book, shoe, etc.

Hold a different object in each hand. Hold the objects at the same height and drop them at the same time. Record observations.

2. Which penny will reach the ground first?

Materials: two rulers, two pennies

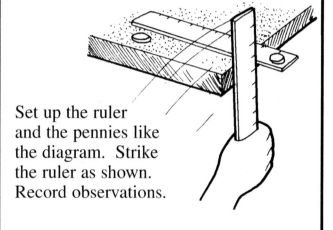

Set up the ruler and the pennies like the diagram. Strike the ruler as shown. Record observations.

3. What happens to the cup?

Materials: paper cups, playing cards

Stack the cups open end down with a card in between each cup. Start at the top and quickly pull out the card between each cup. Record observations.

4. Which coin will reach the ground first?

Materials: 4 different coins, yardstick

Place the coins on the yardstick. Carefully hold the stick over your head and tilt the stick so the coins fall. Record observations.

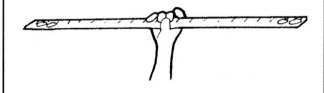

Science Experiments (cont.)

Thrust

Thrust is the force that moves an airplane forward. It creates a flow of fast-moving air that blows in the opposite direction the plane is flying. In order for an airplane to fly, its thrust must be greater than the force of drag which slows it down. Airplane designers try to increase airplane thrust by making powerful jet engines or propellers, and by giving the plane a streamline shape. Try the experiments below to find out how thrust works.

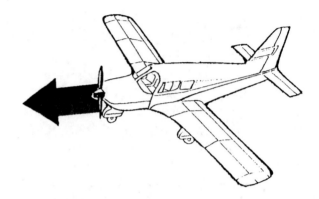

1. Can you blow the ball into the bottle?

Materials: empty soda bottle, small ball of paper

Crush a small piece of paper into a ball smaller than the opening of a soda bottle. Lay the bottle on its side, and put the paper ball just inside the mouth of the bottle. Try to blow the ball into the bottle. Record observations.

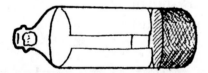

2. What will happen to the fan?

Materials: 6" x 12" board, six round pencils, one electric fan

Lay the pencils in a row on a table. Place the board on the pencils. Put the fan on the board and turn on the fan. Record observations.

3. What will happen to the balloon jet?

Materials: 6 feet of string, tape, balloons, one straw

Run the string through the straw and tie the two ends of the string to two chairs. Pull the chairs apart to make the string taut. Blow up one balloon halfway, and hold the neck closed. Tape the balloon to The straw. Pull the balloon to one chair and let the balloon go. Record how far the balloon jet travels. Repeat the experiment. This time blow up the balloon all the way. How far does this jet go? Why? Tape a new balloon to the straw going in the opposite direction. Repeat experiment. What happens? Why?

56

Science Experiments *(cont.)*

Drag

Drag is the force that pushes against an airplane and slows it down. The shape of an airplane affects the amount of drag. Aircraft engineers try to build planes with low drag because they need less engine power to fly and have better flight performance. The best airplanes have a sleek, trim shape so that they will cut like a knife through the air. All moving objects (humans, cars, trucks, birds) experience drag. Try the experiments below to find out how drag works.

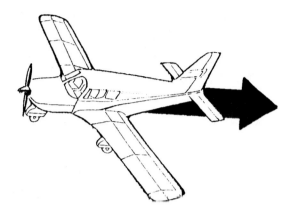

1. Who can run faster?

Materials: large sheet of tagboard

Find a friend to have a running race. One of you hold the piece of tagboard in front of you as you run. Record your observations after the race.

2. Which piece of paper will reach the ground first?

Materials: 2 identical sheets of paper

Crumple one sheet of paper into a ball. Stand and hold the paper ball in one hand and the sheet of paper in the other hand. Hold your hands at the same height and drop the papers at the same time. Record observations.

3. How does a parachute affect an object's fall to the ground?

Materials: yarn, scissors, two clothespins or two large paper clips, hole punch, 8" square sheet of paper or cloth

Cut 4 pieces of yarn 1 foot long. Make one hole in each corner of the paper or cloth square. Tie the pieces of yarn to each corner. Pinch the 4 yarn ends together with the clothespin or tie them to the paper clip. Stand on a chair and hold the clothespin parachute in one hand and the clothespin in the other hand. Drop both from the same height at the same time. Record observations.

Milestones in Flight History

Draw lines to connect the names with their correct contributions to the development of flight. Use an encyclopedia to help you. Then complete the time line on page 59.

Louis Blériot	**1947:** First pilot to fly faster then the speed of sound.
William Boeing	**1932:** Flew solo across the Atlantic Ocean
Albert Santos Dumont	**1804:** Flew the first successful glider
Richard Byrd	**1909:** First person to fly across the English Channel
Amelia Earhart	**1911:** Built first airplanes for the United States Navy
Howard Hughes	**1942:** Led first airplane bombing raid on Tokyo in World War II
Samuel Langley	**1900:** German pioneer who flew his first airship (blimp)
Calbraith Perry Rodgers	**1919:** American industrialist who helped carry the world's first international mail in one of his airplanes
Glenn Curtiss	**1490:** Italian sculptor and painter who first made plans for a flying machine
Otto Lilienthal	**1783:** Made one of the first hot air balloons
Charles Lindbergh	**1890:** Built gliders that could be piloted
Billy Mitchell	**1927:** First aviator to fly non-stop across the Atlantic from New York to Paris
Joseph Montgolfier	**1946:** Army general who wanted an Air Force apart from the Army and Navy
Wiley Post	**1903:** Pioneer in aeronautics who built an "aerodrome"
Igor Sikorsky	**1933:** First to fly around the world alone
Wright Brothers	**1913:** Designed world's first four-engine aircraft
Chuck Yeager	**1940:** Designed and flew the *Spruce Goose*, an eight-engine wooden flying boat
Ferdinand Zeppelin	**1903:** Built and flew the first motor-driven airplane
Leonardo da Vinci	**1906:** Built first successful French airplane
Donald Douglass	**1926:** Made first flight over North Pole
George Cayley	**1924:** American aircraft manufacturer who designed first army planes that flew around the world
James Doolittle	**1911:** Made first transcontinental flight across the United States

Fight Time Line

Complete the time line using information from page 58. (Have your teacher make 3 copies of this page. Tape the copies together excluding the example.)

1490

Name: **Leonardo da VInci**

Contribution: **Made first plans for flying machine.**

Name:

Contribution:

Name:

Contribution:

Name:

Contribution:

Name:

Contribution:

Name:

Contribution:

Name:

Contribution:

Name:

Contribution:

Around the World

Label the seven continents and four major oceans. Read *Lost Star* to find out where Amelia Earhart started her around-the-world flight. Mark this place with an X. Label each place where Amelia landed on her famous journey. Draw a circle where Amelia crashed. Draw a dashed line to show the route she planned to take to finish her trip. Color your map.

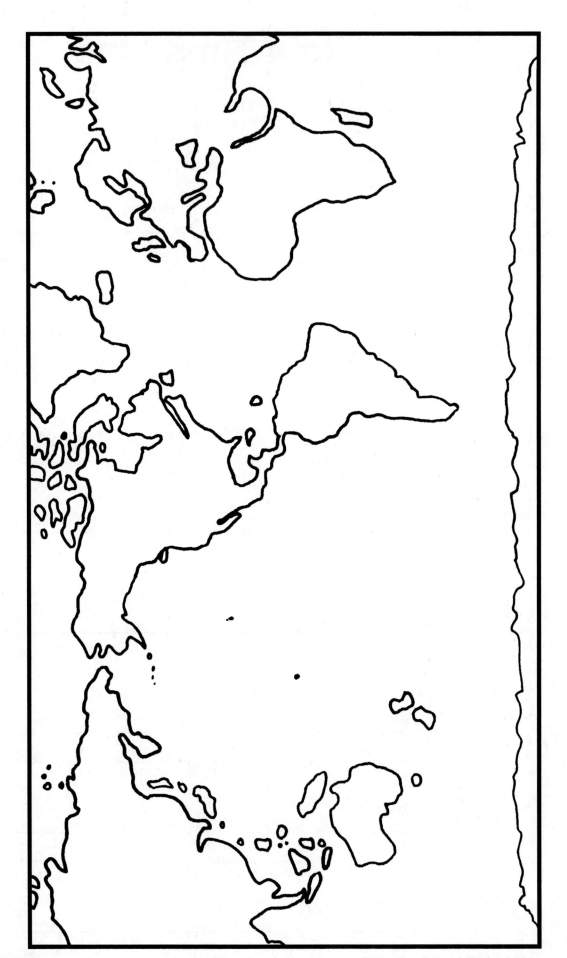

The World's Busiest Airports

- In the chart below, write the country where each airport is located.

- Have your teacher choose one of these ways to organize the airports: Alphabetically; greatest to least number of passenger arrivals/departures; greatest to least number of take-offs/landings; U.S. airports vs. foreign airports.

- Cut out the airport strips along the dashed lines and glue them to a separate sheet of paper in the proper order.

- Afterward, locate and label each airport on a copy of the world map, page 60.

Airport	Passenger Arrivals/Departures	Take-offs/ Landings	Country
1. Logan International (Boston)	20,450,000	347,600	
2. Metropolitan (Detroit)	15,607,000	311,800	
3. Los Angeles International	37,648,000	473,500	
4. Tokyo International	27,167,000	155,700	
5. Heathrow International (London)	31,310,000	288,300	
6. Frankfurt	19,540,000	219,600	
7. Dallas-Fort Worth Regional	37,104,000	534,500	
8. Honolulu International	16,639,000	246,500	
9. Orly International (Paris)	17,671,000	154,900	
10. San Francisco International	24,931,000	345,000	
11. Osaka International	17,452,000	122,700	
12. Chicago-O'Hare International	48,469,000	713,600	
13. Miami International	19,849,000	282,800	
14. La Guardia (New York City)	20,542,000	312,600	
15. Pearson International (Toronto)	15,800,000	219,800	
16. Stapleton International (Denver)	28,486,000	437,300	
17. J.F.K. International (New York)	28,945,000	254,700	
18. Lambert International (St. Louis)	19,942,000	364,000	
19. Hartsfield International (Atlanta)	42,495,000	718,100	
20. Newark Intl. (New York City)	28,577,000	341,700	

Illustrating Reports

Practice each of the following techniques with your class. Then have students choose which technique is appropriate for the picture they want to use in their reports.

Grid Enlargement

Teach students how to enlarge a drawing by using a grid. Make clear overlays of the centimeter grid on page 63. Make normal copies of the 1" grid. Have students place the 1" grid under a white piece of paper. Have them place the centimeter grid overlay on the picture they want to copy. Use paper clips to hold the grids in place. Have students copy what is in the squares on the clear overlay onto the white piece of paper using the 1" squares as a guide.

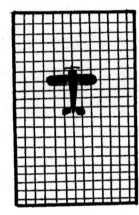 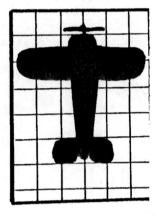

Overhead Transparency

Make a transparency of a picture for the overhead projector. Have students copy the outline of the picture onto paper by keeping their eyes on the picture and not on their papers. Have students add details to complete their pictures.

Right Brain Drawing

Make a copy of a picture for each student. Have students turn the picture upside down and cover the picture with another piece of paper. Have students uncover the picture 1" at a time and draw each portion on another piece of paper. When the picture is completed have students turn it right side up and add details.

 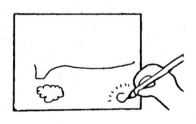

Grids

One-inch grid

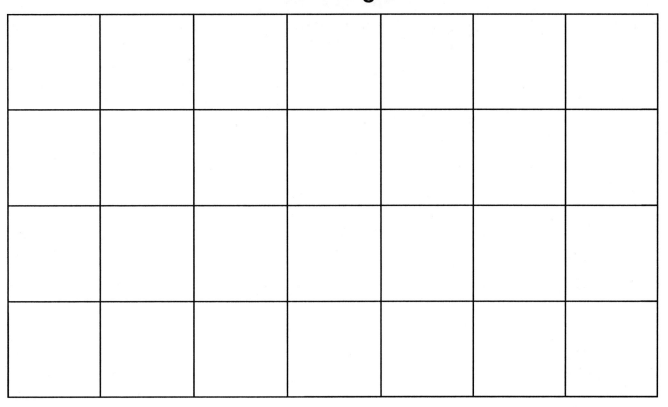

One-centimeter grid

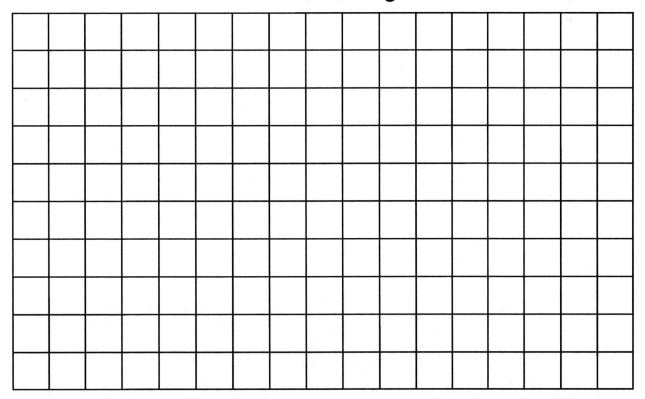

Art Ideas

Sunset Flight

Materials: watercolor paints; brushes; white construction paper; airplane patterns (pages 75–78)

Have students do a watercolor wash using sunset colors on a sheet of construction paper. Instruct students to cut out three patterns of planes: large, medium, and small. Have students glue the patterns onto the dried watercolor paintings.

Oil Painting

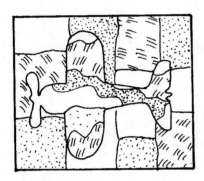

Materials: black construction paper; chalk; white glue; oil pastels

Have students draw the shape of a plane on black construction paper with chalk. Have students draw chalk lines to divide the plane and background into sections. Direct students to go over all lines with white glue. After the glue has dried, have students use oil pastels to color the sections. Have them use warm colors for the plane and cool colors for the background.

Airplane Mobile

Materials: string; coat hanger; scissors; tape; construction paper; airplane patterns (See pages 75–78); colored pencils, markers

Have students make a title for their mobiles on construction paper: *Aircraft, Historical Development, Flight History, Unique Airplanes,* etc. Help students tape their mobile titles to their coat hangers. Have students trace and cut out several airplane patterns. Have students decorate their airplanes with art supplies. Have them cut string into different lengths, and tape one piece of string to the top of each airplane. Help students tape or tie the strings to their mobile titles. Display mobiles in the classroom.

Mural

Materials: butcher paper; construction paper; glue; scissors; chalk; crayons; markers; paints; yarn; fabric scraps; tissue, torn paper, etc.

Have students select a flight topic to depict in a mural using different art supplies. (For topics, see Book Ideas, page 30, or Milestones in Flight History, page 58.) Allow students to decide how they will organize the project to involve every student in the class.

Flight Careers

Many people are needed to help fly an airplane, and many opportunities exist for a career in the flight industry. Use an encyclopedia or dictionary or talk to an expert to learn more about one of these occupations. Write a paragraph in your own words that includes a job description, special education or training, and qualities you think are necessary to be successful at this occupation.

- **FLIGHT ENGINEERS** work on large airplanes. They are in charge of inspecting the planes before take-off. They make sure all systems work properly during the flight.

- **MECHANICS** make sure the airplane's engines and mechanical parts are running properly.

- **METEOROLOGISTS** keep track of weather patterns that will affect the flight of the airplane.

- **CONTROLLERS** direct airplanes at the airport. They tell pilots when and where to take off and land.

- **PASSENGER SERVICE WORKERS** Plan and prepare meals, keep the plane clean, load and unload cargo, sell tickets, and help passengers.

- **OPERATION MANAGERS** keep the airport running smoothly by taking care of any problems that develop.

- **AIRPORT SERVICE WORKERS** are responsible for keeping airplane runways and roads dear, and for providing emergency services.

- **SECURITY OFFICERS** protect people in the airport and watch to keep anyone or anything dangerous away from airplanes and passengers.

- **OTHER FLIGHT OCCUPATIONS:** Airplane designer, dispatcher, pilot, navigator, builder, cargo handler, and travel agent.

Job Application

Teacher Preparation

Make a job chart for your classroom, and write job titles and their descriptions on library book pockets. Insert 3" x 5" cards with the names of students responsible for each job.

Have students apply for different classroom jobs using the application below. This activity is an excellent way to teach students responsibility and leadership skills in the classroom. After they have experience with the form, have them apply for one of the flight careers on page 65.

Student Directions

When applying for a job, neatness and accuracy is very important in filling out the application. Practice writing your answers on a separate sheet of paper and use the form below for your final draft. Use your best handwriting to make a good first impression.

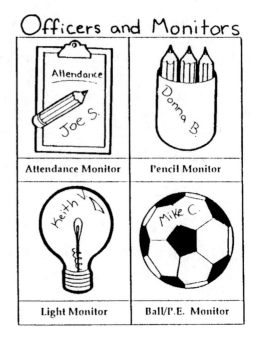

Officers and Monitors

Attendance Monitor   Pencil Monitor

Light Monitor   Ball/P.E. Monitor

Job Application for the position of _____

Name: _____ **Social Security Number:** _____

Street: _____ **School Name:** _____

City: _____ **State:** _____ **Zip Code:** _____

Special Training: (Name two things you know how to do that are related to the job you want.):

1. _____

2. _____

List three friends who would say you are a good person for the job.

1. _____ 2. _____ 3. _____

Give two reasons telling why you want this job.

1. _____

2. _____

On the back of this page, write a short paragraph about yourself. Tell when and where you were born. Describe what you look like. Name three things you like to do.

Special Qualities

Famous people like the Wright brothers and Amelia Earhart have special qualities which help them accomplish what they set out to do. To complete the chart below, select a quality from the list that you think you need to help you do each task. Then choose a famous person who you think has this quality.

Task	Quality	Famous Person
1. Starting and leading a new school club		
2. Cleaning room when you don't want to		
3. Listening to a friend who is upset		
4. Telling truth when you've done wrong		
5. Talking to a new student in class		
6. Doing right though people laugh at you		
7. Taking care of younger brother or sister		
8. Making a unique gift for your parents		
9. Working with friends to build something		
10. Deciding to complete your homework		

Qualities
Compassion
Cooperation
Goal-Setting
Initiative
Honesty
Risk-Taking
Bravery
Patience
Perseverance
Creativity

Famous People
Amelia Earhart
Martin Luther King, Jr.
Daniel Boone
Mother Theresa
Louis Blériot
Abraham Lincoln
Harriet Tubman
Leonardo da Vinci
Wright brothers
Helen Keller

A Day at the Airplane Races

This activity allows students to develop their creativity and social skills while having fun. See page 69 for directions for two paper airplanes, or use these resource books: *Instant Paper Airplanes, 30 Planes for the Paper Pilot,* and *The Ultmate Paper Airplane.* (See Bibliography, page 80.)

Materials

8½" x 11" sheets of paper; scissors; colored pencils, crayons or markers; 6-foot length of yarn or rope

Directions

Explain the different categories of competition to your students. Have each student make an airplane, or have groups each design one paper airplane. Allow time for test flights. Encourage students who are having difficulty by reminding them about Louis Blériot's nine designs before he finally succeeded.

Categories

Endurance: Have the pilots from two groups stand behind a base line with their airplanes. Have the pilots launch their planes. The plane that stays up the longest wins. Have the winners of the groups compete until there is only one winner. (Option: Time the planes with a stopwatch.)

Accuracy: Make a bullseye out of yarn on the ground 25 feet from the base line. The plane closest to the center wins. (Option: Make several concentric rings and assign points for each. Give each group three tries to score.)

Distance: Have pilots from each group launch their planes at the same time from behind the base line. The plane that flies the farthest wins.

Creativity: Have the class vote by secret ballot on the most creative plane.

Speed: Place a finish line 25 yards or more away from the base line. Have two pilots compete at a time. After a pilot launches his plane, he/she runs to the place where it lands, picks it up, and throws it again. Pilots cannot walk or run with their planes to the finish line. The first pilot to throw his/her airplane over the finish line is the winner. (Option: Have an airplane relay race. Have members of each group spread out between the start and finish lines. Each group must try to get its airplane to the finish line by relaying it to its group members.)

Altitude: The student or group with the plane that flies the highest wins. Make awards to give to the winners of each category, and after the races, set up an airplane museum.

Paper Airplanes

Basic Flyer: Use an 8½" x 11" sheet of paper. Fold along dotted lines as shown.

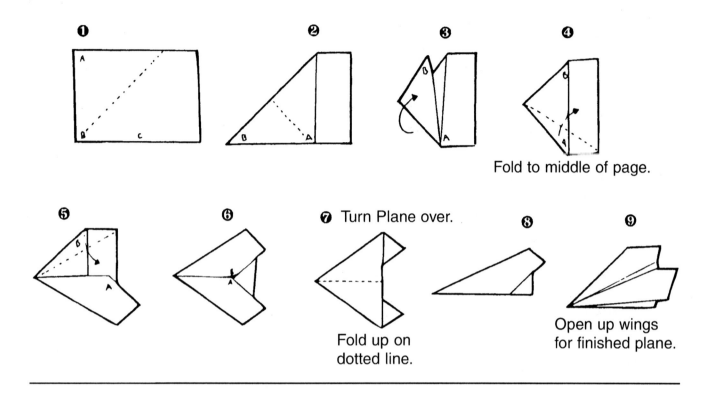

Fold to middle of page.

Turn Plane over.

Fold up on dotted line.

Open up wings for finished plane.

Flying Cylinder: Use a 8½; square sheet of paper. Fold along dotted lines as shown.

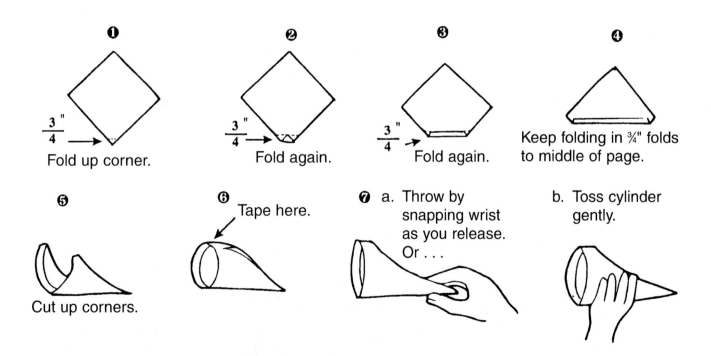

Fold up corner.

Fold again.

Fold again.

Keep folding in ¾" folds to middle of page.

Cut up corners.

Tape here.

a. Throw by snapping wrist as you release. Or . . .

b. Toss cylinder gently.

Challenges *(A student play)*

Have each student play the role of a famous person they researched from Milestones in Flight History, page 58. For rehearsal techniques, see Readers' Theater, page 25.

Class: A dream we all had

Impossible it seemed

But through the good and the bad

We constantly dreamed.

*Player 1: I am _____

I lived _____

I _____

(Player describes his/her contribution to flight. Players 2, 3, and 4 in turn begin at the *.)

Player 1:   Determined I was

Player 2:   For a goal I had set.

Player 3:   I never gave up

Player 4:   'Til my challenge was met!

After these four players have finished their lines, have four new players repeat the procedure starting at the *. Do this until everyone in the class has been involved.

Class: We've told you our dreams

The challenge was ours.

Have each student call out a different character trait for his/her famous person. (For ideas of character traits, see Character Web, page 40, and Special Qualities, page 67.)

PERSISTENCE! DETERMINATION! CURIOSITY! VISION! DEPENDABILITY! COMPASSION! ETC.

Class: All these we had and

Our goals we reached

Now we challenge YOU:

Make it your quest

TO DO YOUR BEST!

Bulletin Board Ideas

Materials: Airplane pattern (page 72); construction paper; scissors; colored markers or crayons; stapler; pushpins

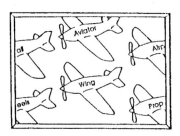

Up, Up and Away

Write flight vocabulary words and their definitions on copies of the plane pattern, page 72. See Word Bank, page 42, for vocabulary.

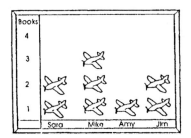

Away We Go

Make a bar graph to show the number of flight books each student has read. Use the airplane pattern on page 72 to represent one book, and put the correct number of planes next to each student's name.

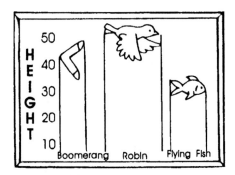

Flying High

Make a giant altitude graph. Have students draw a picture of each flying object from Flying High, page 49. Have them staple their drawings to the correct altitude location on the bulletin board.

Off We Go

Write interesting flight facts next to copies of airplane patterns and display them on a bulletin board. (See Clip Art, pages 75–78).

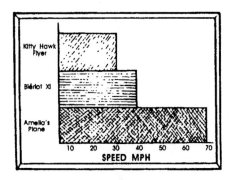

Take-off

Create a bar graph to display the different speeds of airplanes. Use the information from How Much Farther?, page 46 and Distance Graph, page 47.

Bulletin Board Ideas *(cont.)*

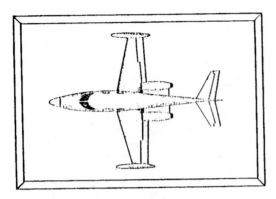

Know Your Airplane!

Enlarge the airplanes from Airplane Parts, page 44, and use 3" x 5" cards to label the parts on a bulletin board.

We Meet The Challenge!

Display good work and achievement awards, pages 73–74. Write compliments on students' papers like "Flying Ace," "Top Gun," "Best Pilot," or "High Flyer."

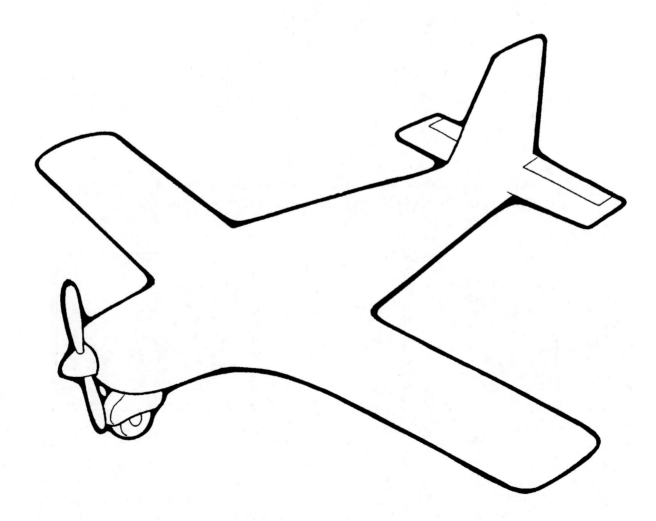

Achievement Awards

The Louis Blériot award for

PERSISTENCE

_____
Name of Student

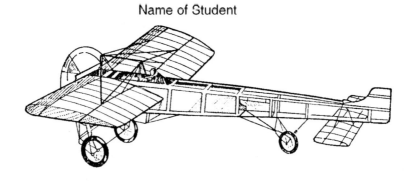

_____
Teacher Signature

_____
Date

The Wright Brothers Award for

COOPERATION

_____
Name of Student

_____
Teacher Signature

_____
Date

Achievement Awards *(cont.)*

_____
Name of Student

receives

The Leonardo da Vinci Award
for

CREATIVITY

in

_____

_____

_____

_____
Teacher Signature

_____
Date

The Amelia Earhart Award for

SETTING and Accomplishing GOALS

Goal(s) accomplished: _____

_____

_____
Name of Student

_____
Teacher Signature

_____
Date

Clip Art

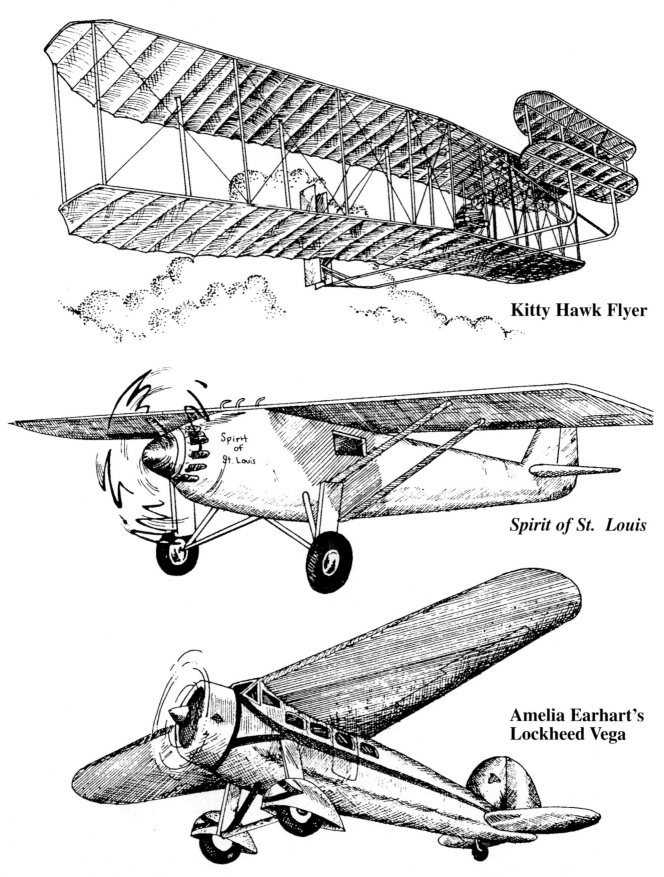

Kitty Hawk Flyer

Spirit of St. Louis

**Amelia Earhart's
Lockheed Vega**

Clip Art *(cont.)*

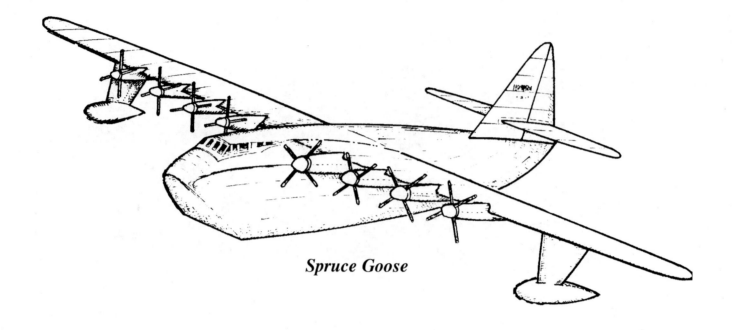

Spruce Goose

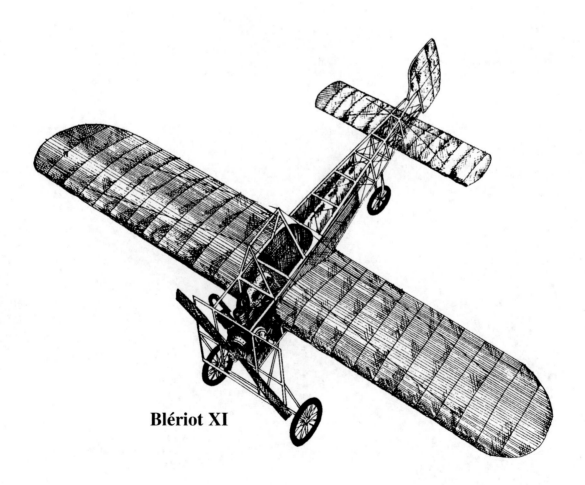

Blériot XI

Clip Art *(cont.)*

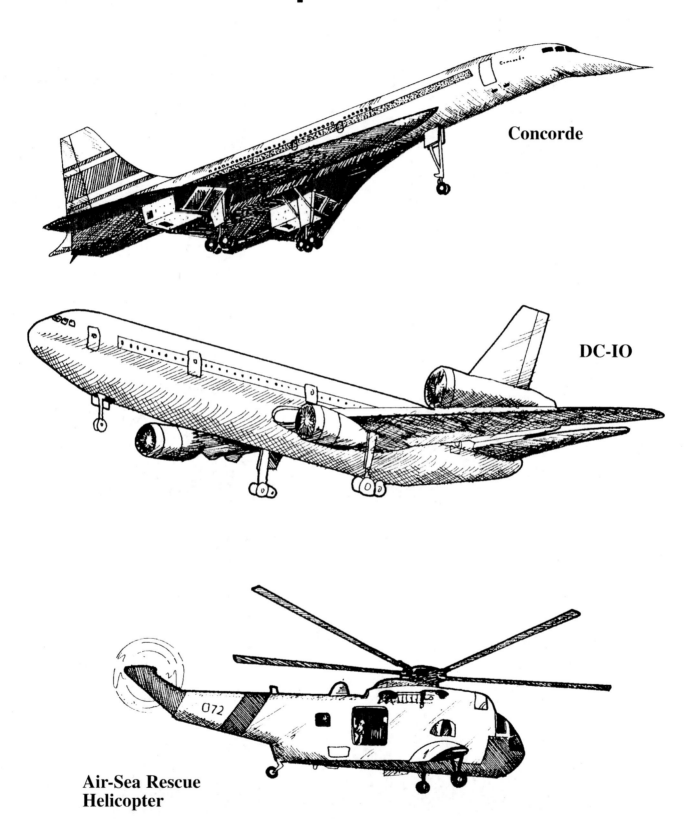

Concorde

DC-IO

Air-Sea Rescue
Helicopter

Clip Art *(cont.)*

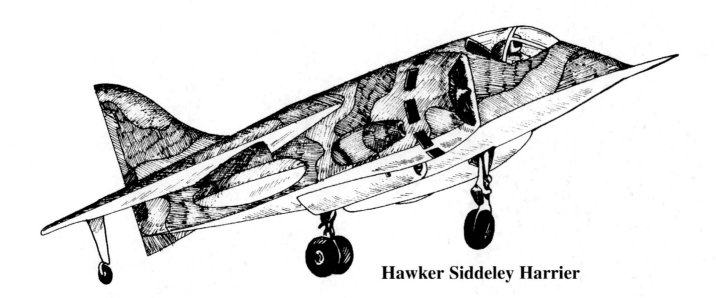

Hawker Siddeley Harrier

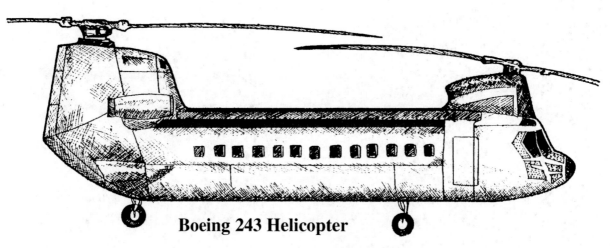

Boeing 243 Helicopter

Lockheed C-5 Galaxy

     78

Answer Key

Page 8
Clue words will vary.
Flyer: 1, 4, 6, 8, 10, 12, 13
Flight: 2, 3, 5, 7, 9, 11, 14

Page 9
1. Mr. Wright was a minister. Mrs. Wright encouraged her children to learn and never told them they couldn't accomplish something even when the boys said they wanted to fly! Wilbur was the oldest brother, then Orville, then Kate.
2. Answers rnight include the brothers' toy designs, schooling, books they read, and adventures they had.
3. They read to each other from books at home and in the library. The loved encyclopedias because they learned new information. They often argued about new ideas and whether or not the information was correct.
4. The Wrights used the library, encyclopedias, the U.S. Weather Bureau, and the Smithsonian.
5. They began with kites and then developed gliders with elevators for better control. They tested more than 1000 gliders each with a slight change before they felt ready to try an engine-powered flying machine.
6. Otto Lilienthal; After many failures the brothers tested his assumptions, which proved to be incorrect. The learned never to assume something without testing it first.
7. The main problem was how to use a heavier-than-air engine in a machine light enough to fly.
8. They flipped a coin.
9. On December 17,1903, Orville took off from a windy beach at Kitty Hawk, North Carolina while five people watched. He flew 120 feet and stayed aloft for 12 seconds.
10. Most did not believe it happened. A few printed a small comment about an unusual occurrence.
11. Answers will vary.
12. Answers will vary. Help students see the benefits of using more than one source of information when doing research. Have students share their answers with one another and add additional inforrnation to their pages.

Page 10
1. Yes, Leonardo's life was filled with the attainment of knowledge.
2. Leonardo's works include: The *Mona Lisa*, *The Last Supper*, and *The Virgin and Child with SaintAnne*
3. Universal means able to do many things. Yes, Leonardo is universal.
4. He made flight designs. Yes, he should be aedited.
5. He wrote his ideas in mirror writing so no one could steal them.

Page 16
Both: Pilots, made famous flights across water, loved flying
Individual:Answers will vary. Refer to biographies.

Page 21
Midnight: *Itasca* turns on its searchlights and sends voice and telegraph messages.

12:30	*Itasca* broadcasts again.
1:15	AE is still not heard from.
1:30	*Itasca* radios, "Please observe schedule with key."
2:45	AE announces that it is cloudy and overcast.
3:00	*Itasca* began sending "A" signal to guide AE.
3:15	AE is not heard from.
3:30	*Itasca* asks AE to report her position.
3:45	AE reports, "Will listen on hour and half hour on 3105."
5:00	AE is heard but not understood.
6:15	AE asks *Itasca* to take bearing on her from her whistle.
6:45	AE's voice comes through clear and strong but too briefly.
7:42	AE says she can't reach *Itasca* by radio and is low on fuel.
7:58	AE says she is circling but cannot hear *Itasca*.
8:45	AE is heard clearly and gives her position. This is the last time AE is heard from again.

Page 38
Airplane—made of honeycomb paper, weighed less than 2000 Ibs., lightweight, non-metal, had 17 fuel tanks
Supplies—7000 Ibs. of fuel, dried foods, 20 gallons of water, bottled oxygen
Flight—Took off Dec. 14, 1986; non-stop flight around the world; flew 25,012 miles; trip took 9 days, 3 min., 44 sec.; landed Dec. 23, 1986.

Page 43
Airplane—Alfa, India, Romeo, Papa, Lima, Alfa, November, Echo
Pilot:—Papa, India, Lima, Oscar, Tango
Weather:—Whiskey, Echo, Alfa, Tango, Hotel, Echo, Romeo
(**Name**):—Answers will vary

Page 44
1. Ailerons 2. Trailing Edge 3. Fuselage
4. Elevators 5. Rudder 6. Fin 7. Wing
8. Leading Edge 9. Windshield 10. Jet Pod
11. Horizontal Stabilizer 12. Landing Gear
13. Tail Light 14. Wing Tip Fuel Tank
15. Air Intake 16. Jet Thrust 17. Wing Span
18. Cabin 19. Landing Light 20. Cabin Door

Page 45
1. 7.9 m 2. 116.4 m 3. 198 feet 4. 503 feet
5. 231 feet 6. 46.4 m

Page 46
Flyer—90, 120, 150; *747*—1250, 1875, 2500, 3125; *BlériotXI*—76, 114, 152, 190; *Concorde*—3100, 4650, 6200, 7750; *Electra*—140, 210, 280, 350; *Shuttle*:—32,000; 48,000; 64,000; 80,000

Page 48
Flyer—90 hrs.; *BlériotXI*—71 hrs., 6 min.; Amelia's first plane—38 hrs., 36 min. *747*:—4 hrs., 18 min.; *Concorde*—1 hr.,42 min.
1. 595 mph; 2. 1480 mph; 3. 693 mph;
4. 2245 mph; 5. 925 mph

Page 49

Name	Feet	Miles	Kilometers	Meters
Jet	36,960	7	11.2	11,200
Helicopter	42,240	8	12.8	12,800
Cirrus Clouds	21,120	4	6.4	6,400
Whistling Swan	5,280	1	1.6	1,600
Verreaux Eagle	5,280	1	1.6	1,600
Space Shuttle	897,600	170	272	272,000
Unmanned Balloon	142,560	27	43.2	43,200
Two-Passenger Plane	15,840	3	4.8	4,800

1. Space Shuttle 2. *Whistling Swan, Verreaux Eagle* 3. 26,400 4. *Swan, Eagle* 5.170

Page 51
Answers will vary. 1. Sun 2. Moon 3. Answers willvary 4. Answers will vary

Page 52
Scientist:-Asks questions, does experiments to find answers; **Experiment**-Way to find out why something happens; **Research**-Investigating and gathering facts about a subject; **Data**-Information; **Scientific Method**-orderly method of research; **Hypothesis**-Explanation of what will happen; **Procedure**-Step-by-step way of doing things; **Results**-outcome of experiment; **Conclusion**-Final decision about what happened

Answer Key *(cont.)*

Page 54

1. Paper should fit upward. 2. Card should be lifted by suction from funnel. 3. Stamp should lift and stick to quarter. 4. Poke hole through bottom of cup with pencil; put up over paper; suck air through hole to lift paper.

Page 55

1. Objects will fall at same rate. 2. Pennies will reach ground at same time. 3. Cups won't fall. (Force of gravity is greater than pulling force). 4. Coins will reach ground at same time.

Page 56

1. Paper ball should pop out of bottle. Air pushes it from behind. 2. Fan should roll on board over pencils. 3. Balloon jet should travel along string. Full balloon should travel farther because it has more thrust. 4. New balloon will propel jet in opposite direction because thrust is in opposite direction.

Page 57

1.Boy without tagboard will run faster because he has less drag. 2.Crumpled paper will reach ground first because it has less drag to slow it down. 3.Parachute will fall slower because it has more drag.

Page 58

Leonardo da Vinci - 1490; Montgolfier - 1783; Cayley - 1804; Lilienthal - 1890; Zeppelin - 1900; Wright Bros. - 1903 (Built and flew . . .); Langley - 1903 (Pioneer in . . .); Dumont - 1906; Blériot - 1909; Curtiss - 1911; Rodgers - 1913 (Made first transcontinential flight . . .); Sikorsky - 1913 (Designed world's first . . .); Boeing - 1919; Douglass - 1924; Byrd - 1926; Lindbergh - 1927; Earhart - 1932; Post - 1933; Hughes - 1940; Doolittle - 1942; Mitchell - 1946; Yeager - 1947

Page 60 See map at right. ➡

Page 61

U.S.—1, 2, 3, 7, 8, 10, 12, 13, 14, 16, 17, 18,19,20; Japan—4,11; England—5; Germany—6; France—9;Canada—15.

Page 67

Answers will vary. Here are some possibilities:

1. Initiative: Tubman 2. Perseverance: Blériot 3. Compassion: Mother Theresa 4. Honesty: Lincoln 5. Risk-Taking: Daniel Boone 6. Bravery: King 7. Patience: Keller 8. Creativity: da Vinci 9. Cooperation: Wright Bros. 10. Goal-Setting: Earhart

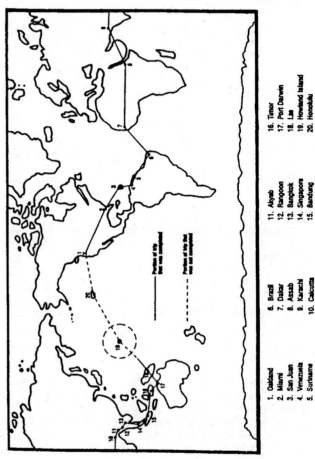

Bibliography

Bendick, Jeanne. *The First Book of Airplanes.* (Franklin Watts, 1976).

Berliner, Don. *Record Breaking Airplanes.* (Lerner, 1985).

Chadwick Roxanne. *Amelia Earhart.* (Lerner, 1987).

Churchill, Richard E. *Instant Paper Airplanes.* (Sterling, 1988).

Collins, David. *Charles Lindbergh.* (Garrard, 1978).

Frachere, Ruth. *The Wright Brothers.* (Thomas Crowell, 1972).

Gilleo, Alma. *Air Travel from the Beginning.* (Children's Press, 1977).

Highland, Harold Joseph. *Airplanes and the Story of Flight.* (Grosset & Dunlap, 1974).

Hook, Jason. *The Wright Brothers.* (Bookright, 1989).

Johnson, Spencer. *The Value of Patience-The Story of the Wright Brothers.* (Value, 1975).

Kaufman, John. *Voyager.* (Enslow, 1989).

Kline, Richard. *The Ultimate Paper Airplane.* (Simon and Schuster, 1986).

Parlin, John. *Amelia Earhart.* (Garrard, 1962).

Reynolds, Quentin. *The Wright Brothers.* (Random, 1981).

Robbis, Jim. *The Story of Flight.* (Warwick, 1989).

Rosenblum, Richard. *Wings: The Early Years of Aviation.* (Four Winds, 1980).

Stein, Conrad. *The Story of Flight at Kitty Hawk.* (Children's Press, 1980).

Taylor, Richard. *The First Flight.* (Franklin Watts, 1990).

Vollheim, Peter. *30 Planes for the Paper Pilot.* (Pocket Books, 1985).

Yang, Thay. *Exotic Paper Airplanes.* (Cypress House Press, 1991).